The Exchange Life

HOW TO THRIVE IN YOUR
HOST COUNTRY AND NOT JUST SURVIVE

ANDY SERNA

"Exchange isn't a year in your life,

It's a life in a year."

Table of Contents

My story

After my senior year of high school, I made the ambitious decision to leave my country, friends, and family, for 10 months and go to Italy for a cultural exchange through a program called the Rotary Youth Exchange. On September 4th, 2015, I left everything behind, and little did I know this would not only just be a journey of a lifetime, but *the* journey of my lifetime.

Many disagreed. Friends, counselors, and even teachers back home questioned why I would "waste a year of my life" while I could be going to college and begin working in a secure stable job as soon as possible. Therefore, I often heard the question, "Why did you choose to do this exchange?" This was not an easy question to answer. For me, the question had a deeper meaning. I needed to figure out the direction of my life before I could be prepared to answer the question

Therefore, I began with a question of my own: "What is the purpose of my life?" Sigmund Freud says in his book *Civilization and its Discontents* that this question has been asked countless times without receiving a satisfactory answer. He goes on saying that we must turn to the less ambitious question: "What do people demand out of life and wish to achieve in it?" The answer to this question is simple… happiness.

People strive for happiness. We want to become happy and to remain so, and the only way to make the adventurous spirit within me happy is to never stop chasing and creating new experiences and opportunities in my life. That's why I chose to do this exchange.

My whole life, I have constantly searched for new opportunities for myself and am truly afraid of routine. Not only did I gain a better understanding of the world around me, but I grew and matured as a person as well. I created a whole new road on my journey to happiness. Other than picking up the language and integrating the culture as part of my own, I learned to accept and appreciate diversity, gained knowledge I can't acquire from reading books, and created memories that others only dream of creating.

I was stuck in this country with no way of going back. I repeated my senior year of high school and basically tried to create this whole new life in a place where I knew nothing about the language, culture, customs, or traditions. No one had ever seen me before or even heard of me, and to make things worse they weren't the best at speaking English either. So I only had one option, and that was to either take the initiative and do whatever I can to make this experience the best experience of my life, or I could be a victim to life's challenging obstacles in front of me and ruin a perfectly good opportunity to learn tremendously about myself and the world around me.

I decided to contact many past exchange students and ask them all kinds of questions to try to gain some knowledge and put the pieces together on how I could create the best year of my life while on my exchange.

I heard of many stories and even knew some people that did not want to continue their year abroad because they did not enjoy it for whatever reason. They were stuck and wanted to go back home to their friends and families. I did not want this to be me.

I had gained some valuable knowledge through the 4 exchange students I had hosted in the past, my brother who went to Denmark on his exchange the year before I did mine, and by just talking to many more exchange students within the Rotary International community. I applied this knowledge on my year abroad and learned many new things as I went on with my year.

After applying what I knew had worked, and avoiding what I knew didn't work I can honestly say that my exchange year could not have gone any better. Everything was perfect looking back on it. Of course, I had faced certain challenges throughout the way, but I managed to overcome them and create better opportunities for myself because of them.

I feel I have valuable information to pass down to many other struggling exchange students trying to find their place in their new country. And that is why I decided to write this book. This is an experience you should cherish for your lifetime, and so I want to do whatever I can in my power to help you succeed and create the best year you will ever live in your life. I want you to thrive in your host country and not just survive.

The decision to do an exchange year was by far the best decision I have ever made, and I want it to be yours too.

What is an Exchange Student

Before diving into the rules I followed to make my exchange life better than my actual life back home, I think it's wise to examine the term "exchange student" as the definition I have personally created and will be using for the course of the book.

Exchange student: Anyone temporarily living or studying abroad for the purpose of a cultural or academic exchange. Specifically, but not limited to, 10-12 months through exchange programs such as Rotary, Intercultural Exchange, AFS, etc...

This is the definition we will use when we say *exchange student* in the book. Of course, you can be someone studying abroad for a semester or short term through a university and this book will still be applied to you. Just interpret it as though I am talking to you. We are doing this for the sake of limiting all redundancy and inefficiency throughout the book.

How to Read and Use This Book

While this book can certainly be read in a few sittings. I encourage you to look through the table of contents and skip around to the chapters you need help with most in your situation right now. Once you fully grasp that one area (or few areas), go back to the beginning and read from beginning to end as the chapters' order are purposefully designed in the way they are. Feel free to always just skip to the chapters most relatable to your life at that specific moment. Just keep the book with you at all times, because situations will arise during your year where you will need to go back and re-read that specific part you need help with at that time. That's the way I believe will best help you.

In each chapter, I begin by telling you what you need to do in order to successfully master that topic. After that, I begin by telling you my experiences with it and how you can take what worked for me, and learn from what didn't.

Before we begin, let me remind you, we are on this journey together. I have experienced situations exchange students have gone through first hand and will provide you with the best possible information that will allow you to live the best possible year of your life. All these suggestions are based solely off my own personal experience throughout the years are not backed by any scientific research. There is no one answer that fixes all problems. You are just going to have to trust my judgement and read the book with an open mind.

There are thousands of situations that can arise on exchange and every situation is different. So, to completely cover it all would be unrealistic and unreasonable. That is why I will always try my best to answer any questions you have for me if you contact me personally. You can contact me personally through my email or social media accounts that I will leave for you at the end of the book.

Without further ado, here are some tactics that can be universally applied to all exchange student to help them thrive in their year abroad, and not just survive.

Enjoy!

Chapter 1: Entering your host country - The correct Mindset

Leaving your friends, family, and normal daily routine to live in your new host country can be very overwhelming and daunting for almost all exchange students beginning their trip in their new country. You feel scared, uncomfortable, and don't know what to expect on your new journey alone. It's perfectly fine to feel like this in the beginning when saying goodbye to your friends and family leading up to the first few days of your exchange, but do not let these emotions of fear and uncertainty have an effect on you for more than a few days. I know the first couple of months on your exchange are notorious for being the most difficult, but that's what makes the beginning portion of your exchange by far the most critical. It sets the tone for the rest of your exchange and gets you that momentum needed to create the exchange life you imagine for yourself.

Try your best to get rid of these negative emotions in your head and create new emotions of excitement, enthusiasm, and positivity because you are about to create the most fulfilling exchange life you can possibly imagine for yourself. Any sense of doubt or worry will literally keep you from living the exchange life you want to live. It keeps you from making the most of the situation you're currently in and keeps you from taking advantage of the opportunities you so desperately need in the beginning to set the foundation of your exchange. This is when people are most willing to help you,

1

meet you, and be your friend. If you don't act on these opportunities they are very hard to recover from later on.

If you haven't heard this before, let me be the first to tell you this:

Your exchange year is what you make out of it. You get out EXACTLY what you put in.

So what do you need to do?

What you need to do is change your mindset on exchange. Entering your host country with the proper mindset will skyrocket your success in creating the life you want.

You need to truly believe that you are about to live the best year of your life and only you can determine how great of a year it is going to be. Get rid of all negative emotions in your head and attack your year believing that you are worthy of your host family's love and friend's friendship.

Every single time you meet someone new whether it's just another student or adult, make sure to introduce yourself with enthusiasm. This is very important because in the beginning, most students don't know the native language so the way other people get a read on you is all through your body language. They sense the excitement, passion, sadness or happiness you are feeling just by your body language and facial expressions. Whether you are doing this in your native or host language always greet someone with a smile on your face and show them that you are happy to meet them and that you are happy you are in their country. First impressions are so important and it's really hard to give off a good first impression if you are not familiar with their language. That's why showing excitement and enthusiasm is important, because you can be anywhere in the world, and people will still be able to understand your communication through body language.

I understand some of you, for example, many Europeans entering an English speaking country, already know English and so it is easier for you to use your body language and conversational skills to help with these first impressions because you are already confident in yourself. For everybody else that does not know the language, you need to take advantage of the enthusiasm you bring to the table and show with your body language that you are excited and grateful for the opportunity you are given to be there in that host country when you first meet new people.

Even if you try to introduce yourself in their own language and get it wrong, this is still way better than doing it in your own language. It shows you are putting yourself out there and making a commitment to learn their language and immerse yourself in their culture. When people notice this they will tend to like you more and want to help you. This is also true for any other time you are speaking to someone, not just when you are introducing yourself. If they see you give an effort in learning their language, almost all the time they will respect your effort. These first impressions are very important. So much so that I talk way more in depth about them in Chapter 4.

The whole point of what I am trying to tell you is to change your attitude to make yourself more approachable and well-liked because life on exchange becomes a lot easier when people enjoy your presence and want to be around you. It definitely won't define your happiness abroad, but it sure will help it. How you approach people is completely based off your mindset. If you are confident in yourself and go introduce yourself to someone new without hesitation, it shows character and the high value you place on yourself. If you are scared and timid and try to introduce yourself without any confidence because you are scared of rejection or what others might think of you, they will sense it and won't necessarily go out of their way to become your friend. Just put yourself in the other person's shoes. If someone slowly and awkwardly comes up to you that is avoiding eye contact and is speaking in a really soft voice tries to become your friend, how much more likely are you willing to go out of your way to be their friend than the next person that comes up to you with a smile and a loud confident voice radiating happiness and positive energy? If you had to choose, you'd probably go with the more enthusiastic and positive person.

Any sort of emotion you are feeling I guarantee people will sense it. If someone criticizes you because of your culture and discourages you because you are not very good at speaking their language and you begin to get these negative thoughts running through your mind, you will start to feel sorry for yourself and your actions will be affected. You might experience telling yourself things like "coming here was a bad idea", "these people will never like me", or "I'm going to be alone the whole year" and once you do that you have already lost. You feel sorry for yourself and begin to live in a state of resentment and regret. You will keep yourself from experiencing many things and meeting many people. And if you do meet people you will give off a bad impression and the chances to recover from a bad first impression are slim. Instead, if you maintain your positive mindset, people will be attracted to it and will want to be around you.

4

One tip I would use that greatly helped me is I would criticize myself and make fun of myself with the other people. So if one of my friends jokingly said, "Damn, your Italian sucks". I would laugh with them and say, "I know I am the worst Italian speaker in the world." This does a few things. It shows you are confident enough in yourself to show everyone you don't care what they think of you. And it shows you are cool enough to take a joke which will make them more comfortable around you. It also shows you are a down to earth personable individual that isn't taking everything to serious, and people love that.

Now if people keep this up, and are just flat out being rude and inconsiderate of your background and culture on a consistent basis, then there is no need to have them in your life. Drop them and don't interact with them anymore. You don't need these people in your life under any circumstance. Your time abroad is limited and should not be wasted around people who do not appreciate you. There will be people that appreciate you, so don't spend your time around the people that bring you down. This is a problem for many exchange students because many are so desperate in finding a friend group, especially when they don't have many other friends in the beginning of the year. But if you ever find yourself in this situation just remember this: No company is better than bad company.

The beginning is very hard for exchange students, but one thing you will find is that the people who do succeed in the beginning are the confident people that generally don't care what anyone thinks of them. That's because they constantly put themselves out there whether they know the language or not, and risk looking stupid in front of everyone - and that's the key. By not caring what other people think you feel less restricted and limited to what you want to say and do, and you are more inclined to step out of your comfort zone and put yourself in situations where you can meet new people and gain more experiences.

You have to take advantage of any opportunity to meet people and experience new things right from the start. Those opportunities will lead to more and more just like a snowball effect, and the sooner you take advantage of them, the sooner you will enjoy you will start to enjoy your exchange. So don't be afraid to put yourself out there, I promise you the potential rewards will be far greater than the feeling of being said 'no' too.

One quote I try to live by, and I recommend you write down to remind yourself when times get tough is this.

You will reach a *dangerous* level of freedom, once you truly stop caring what other people think of you.

Don't get confused with what I am trying to tell you. You still need to try and get on peoples good sides by getting them to want to be around you and hang out with you because that is very important on your exchange. But only once other peoples' opinions of you start having a drastic effect on how you're living your life is when you need to revert back to this statement and remind yourself that you deserve better. I'm not asking you to change, I'm just asking you to bring out the better version of yourself for everyone to see. You are after all, capable of such things, or you wouldn't be in a completely different country alone for a year if you weren't.

Summary:

- Always keep that positive enthusiastic mindset when you first meet people and are approaching a new circumstance.

- Don't allow people to negatively affect your emotions and make you feel bad for yourself by making you feel like you don't belong. Don't allow others' opinions to become your reality.

- Step out of your comfort zone and put yourself in situations to learn, grow, and create relationships with others around you. Those opportunities will lead to others.

My experience:

Before going into my exchange I had already read many self-help books. Not because I was doing the exchange, but because I've always just wanted to grow into a better person and improve myself daily. Many of the books I read had talked about how your attitude and mindset toward everything will determine the outcome of your life. After reading that for the first time I thought "yeah whatever" and didn't think too much of it. As I continued reading book after book, I realized this theme was present everywhere, and so I decided to implement it. I started becoming more proactive and less reactive. I centered my focus and attention to things I was able to control, and didn't react or worry too much about things out of my control. *And that was the key.* Not reacting and giving attention to things that didn't deserve my attention. After months of working on it, it became to be a part of who I was. I was naturally focusing only on things I could change and was happier because of it. And because I was happier I was more enthusiastic about what I did. This, combined with the confidence I taught myself through constant self-improvement was a recipe for success.

When I got to my host country, I literally had no idea what to expect. I didn't know if people would like me, if I would have a great time, or if I would learn the language, but what I did know was that all of those things were in my control. When I arrived, I made sure I was extremely polite and excited to meet everyone I came in contact with. My goal was to leave every single person I met with an impression, like "wow, I like this guy. He is pretty cool", even though they knew nothing about me. I would introduce myself with confidence, look everybody in the eye, and try my absolute best to remember their names when they told me them. When someone was in the room and no one had introduced us, I would always go and introduce myself. I tried to make myself believe that everyone wanted to become friends with an exchange student. I engraved into my mind that people wanted to meet me, and that I was cool enough to be friends with everybody. I basically tricked myself into thinking I was good enough for everyone. Not in a cocky way, but in a confident way, there is a huge difference. Once I programmed my mind to think like that, I started acting accordingly, and I quickly met so many people. I knew what I was going to get out of this exchange was exactly what I put into it. I looked for any single opportunity to leave the house and just do something, whether it was by myself, my host parents, or a friend. I wanted to experience everything and do anything I could because that's when everything starts to align. You go out, you meet people, you become friends, and next time they might ask you to hang out with them. Then you go out with them and repeat the process. Even if it is just leaving and getting something to eat or drink by yourself or with your family, you familiarize yourself with your surroundings, and things seem to get less scary from there.

By no means was it easy for me to go up and talk to people I had never met before. I was always scared to go up to someone and introduce myself, but I knew I had to do it anyway. For example, during the second week of school, I was with one of my friends from class and we went to go walk around the school during the two-hour break. He stopped to talk to a group of girls, and I was there waiting for him expecting him to just say hi and continue walking with me right after. Instead, he stayed talking to them for a couple of minutes and I kept my distance just waiting for him to finish the conversation. I was a few meters away looking from a distance and right beside me were a group of guys I could hear talking and joking around with each other. They were loud and kept laughing and playing jokes with each other. I stood there thinking, "Damn those seem like cool guys". Then I thought, wait a minute, what the heck am I doing? I need to go introduce myself. I kept telling myself, "what's the worst that could happen?". Even though I was trying to think this, I was still very intimidated and scared. I was very hesitant to go, but I somehow mustered up the courage to go say hi. So, I went straight into the group and said, "Hey guys, my name is Andy!". I said it just like that, in English, so they could realize I wasn't from there and they could start asking me questions.

I introduced myself, and my friend comes back to me from talking to his group of girlfriends and tells me, that this was the group of guys he wanted me to meet earlier (because he had talked about them once before to me). It turned out that a couple of guys in that group of four, had just done their exchange through Rotary in America the year before. This was their first year back in school, and my friend wanted me to meet them.

So, we immediately started talking and clicked instantly. We talked during that whole break and even met up after school to finish talking. One of the guys, Giovanni, who had done his exchange the year before in New York, invited me and the other exchange students in the city to have a big dinner later that week in his house so we could all hang out and he could meet the rest of them. It ended up being that whole group of guys and all of us exchange students and we all hit it off. We had that dinner, and we became super close. That ended up being my friend group for the rest of the year. I became so close to Giovanni that later down the line his family ended up hosting me as my second family, and he would later become my host brother during the last half of my exchange!

It's honestly crazy how things work out. Those guys were my go-to group of Italian friends I would have with me for the rest of my exchange. They helped me learn the language, and helped me integrate myself into the culture. They knew exactly what I was going through, because some of them had experienced it as well the year before, and they wanted to make sure I was happy on my exchange. I owe a huge part of my success on my exchange to that group of guys. Most of my memories on my exchange came with them.

And yes, you could make the case that I would have most-likely met them later down the line, if I didn't go out of my way to meet them that day, because my city was so small and we all went to the same school. But just because it was like that for me doesn't mean it's going to be like that for you. Go out and introduce yourself to people. I guarantee you will probably meet your best friends like that, just like I did.

Chapter 2: Getting along with your host family

One of the most important things to know when entering your exchange is that it is extremely important to get on your host family's good side. Your situation with your host family could very well make or break your experience as an exchange student.

First off, I just want to say I know when it comes to your host family some get luckier than others. Some exchange students have nice lenient parents with cool host siblings that are your age and some people might get a host family that deep down doesn't even want them in the first place. This is one area in your exchange where luck does play a major factor. But the people in your host family are more likely than not, normal people, which means you can win them over if at first they don't like you.

For example, people love when others show interest in them and when others actually care about them. Ask questions to members of your host family like "how was your day" or "how are you feeling today" that show you care about them. After that continue on the conversation and ask more specific follow-up questions according to what they say to learn more about them and what they are going through. Show them you're really interested and listen carefully so that next time in a conversation if you bring up what they told you before they will see that you were actually listening and remember what they told you. If they see that you are a good listener they will come to you with more of their problems and want to talk to you more. This builds trust and will instantly create a stronger bond between you and them. We will talk more about this in Chapter 4.

This is specifically important for your siblings. You want your siblings to see you as a friend as well. You want them to come to you whenever they need comfort or someone to talk to. Try to be that source for them and provide them with the friendship and love they can come home too after a long day of school. You want them to think of you as a best friend or brother/sister to come home to and not just an exchange student. And if you have younger siblings, they will most definitely look up to you and see you as a role model. You have the opportunity to be that inspiration for them that they are seeking so early in their lives. I remember looking up to the exchange students we hosted when I was a kid. I looked up to them and always wanted them to like me. You have the power to change their lives since they are so young and are absorbing everything around them with such intensity. Plus, if your siblings really like you, especially your younger ones, then by default your parents will like you. This is important to remember. There is a direct correlation to the happiness of your younger siblings and the happiness to your parents. If your parents see that your younger siblings really like you and you are getting along really well with them then your host parents will most likely like you more as well.

With anybody in your family, however, you should remember to have the mindset that no matter how long you are staying there, you are still their guest. You are in their home, and they make the rules. So, it is still your job to be as respectful and considerate as possible. Anything you want to do in their house that you are not sure if you are allowed to do, you must ask. Even if you are pretty sure they will let you, still ask. It shows you are considerate enough of their home and their expectations. If you want to eat food out of the refrigerator and you're not sure whose it is, ask them. Even if they tell you to eat whatever you want. You might say something like, "I know you said I can eat whatever I want, but I was still wondering if I can eat this piece of cake? I just wanted to make sure you weren't planning on eating it later or saving it for anybody." Things like this show you are considerate and are thinking of other people's needs before your own. Or if you want to play the guitar for example, go out and ask everybody if it's ok to play the guitar, to make sure the loud noise doesn't bother them. These are things I did on my exchange and my host family really appreciated this because it showed I was thinking about them before I did anything that could potentially be obnoxious to anyone in the household.

This is an important tactic, because when it comes to having problems with your family many exchange students experience resentment and hostility from their family members out of nowhere. That is because they are releasing built-up long term tension that they have kept hidden from all the little things you may have done that might have set them off. It's rarely the big things you do in a household and usually the many little things you do that could get someone living with you to feel resentment towards you. People tend to hold these feelings of the small little things that anger them, and over time this anger builds up. That is why you may experience people going off on you for no reason at all or for something so small that makes no sense at all.

Always be considerate and polite. Ask questions you're not sure the answers to and put your host family's needs and feelings before yours. If you do, you should be headed down the right path.

14

An important thing I believe you should do as well, is to not spend too much time in your room. You should be trying to create close bonds and a greater relationship with the members of your family, and you can't do that by being locked away in your room the whole time. If you lock yourself in your room for hours at a time consistently, it gives off the message that you don't want to be around your host family and comes off as rude. From personal experience, I have seen and heard of many exchange students that are always in their room for long periods of time every single day. It's very common for exchange students and it doesn't help you become closer to your family. You should be out in the living room hanging out with them or helping them clean around the kitchen. Talk to them and spend more time with them. They will appreciate your presence and will be glad you are spending time with them around the house. Not only will it allow you to build a closer relationship with them, but if you are speaking in your host language as well, you will learn the language so much quicker. That time you would normally spend in your room sleeping or watching Netflix would be used to actually speak the language and will give you that extra practice to become more fluent in your host language.

Something else you can do with your family that would give them a great first impression of you is to bring them personalized gifts from your country back home. I know this is already very common and many people already do this. I highly encourage you to bring a bunch of little gifts for each one of your family members. Bring them souvenirs like shirts, mugs, flip flops, or anything that represents your home country. For example, a shirt with a Brazilian flag if you're from Brazil. A coffee mug that says "Barcelona" if you're from Barcelona. Anything that only you can get from your country, city, or region would be ideal. For example, I am from Texas, and I knew my host brother really liked western movies and comics because I asked him what he liked before I left on my exchange. He told me, so I brought him a western toy pistol and a cowboy hat as a couple of gifts for him and he absolutely loved it! Gifts show your thoughtfulness and care you have for your host family, and I know they would they would really appreciate it. This is a great way to make a good first impression on them.

However, no matter how hard you try there are still some families that may be impossible to deal with. If after some time and effort of trying whatever you can think of to get along with your family and you are still not on the right page, then I would highly suggest talking to Rotary or whoever your exchange counselor is about a change. The reason for this is because your host family could very well make or break your exchange. And if they find nothing wrong with your host family, to the point where they can't accept your change request, then you're just going to have to make the most of it and hope for the best. After all, this whole process is a learning experience, and having a difficult time overcoming challenges only means that in the end, you are going to become a better, wiser person because of it. I have heard of many people not liking their host families and have come out of the situation a better person because of it.

If you do happen to get unlucky and really don't like your host family and they are just not good people to you for whatever reason; and you've talked to your exchange program and done everything you possibly could to change your family and can't do anything about the situation, there are a couple of things you can do to try and ease the pain. First, I would suggest spending more time outside the house and hanging around people you actually do enjoy spending time with, like the other exchange students. Understand that the other exchange students you are with are a GREAT support system for when you are going through hard times during your exchange. They understand exactly where you are coming from and will do anything to help you. They can even talk to their host family about it, who can even be there to help you as well by inviting you over for their own family dinners and by inviting you over to just hang around the house whenever you feel uncomfortable at your own home.

Second, and this is more of a last resort kind of thing, if you need to use your room as an escape from your awful family, then that's ok too. Keep yourself sane as much as you can. If your host family drives you nuts, just grab a nice book to read, put on a nice movie, or study your host language in your room and enjoy the time to yourself. Try to be productive, but do anything you may have to, to keep you from going insane. If you let your host family affect your mood at home, that mood can translate to your world outside your home and in school, and that would be a very bad thing to happen. You don't want your host family to be the reason why you aren't enjoying your exchange outside of your home too.

While there are host families that are very difficult to live with, however, I have found many of them act this way because of the exchange student they are hosting. Therefore, before you blame anyone else or start pointing fingers I highly suggest you look in the mirror and make sure you are not the problem first. This is very difficult to do because we are all biased towards ourselves. You have to be brutally honest with yourself, even if it means admitting things you may not like to admit. Not many people out there choose to be angry for no reason at all. While there are naturally grumpy and disrespectful people out there, there aren't many of them. The chances you might even be paired up with people like this become even more slim, as programs such as Rotary, try to avoid sending students to these kinds of people. So, before you think your host family is the problem try to figure out what you can do

17

better, that might be making them act a certain way. If they naturally just don't like you for no reason at all, then I would definitely suggest talking to someone in charge of your situation.

All that aside, there are also many great host families that want nothing, but the best for their exchange students. No matter who you end up with though, you can always get them to like you if you're just polite and considerate enough. It may not get them to change certain rules within their household, but they won't be so quick to get mad or even punish you if you do end up doing something wrong in the future. Life will just be a lot easier if you and your host family get along. Therefore, try to do anything you can in your power to gain a stronger relationship with your host family.

I have heard many different specific problems students have had with their families and to write about each single problem would take another book, so if you have specific questions get in touch with your program exchange officers from your district in your host country, and if that doesn't work contact the exchange officers from your district back home. If they don't help you for whatever reason, contact me personally about your specific problem and I will try to help you solve your problem or lay out the different options you may have to take. Even if you just need someone to talk to, to try and get you through it I am here for that. However, there are also a bunch of people on Facebook or social media that have been through the exact same problems you have and would love to help you too so you don't have to go through what they did. When going to someone for help about a specific situation, I highly suggest finding someone who has been through the same situation you're going through. You may be able to learn exactly from what they did, which will cut the learning curve for you and tell you what next steps you should take. Contacting someone else saves time which is very important since your time abroad is very limited. But always go to the higher-ups first, to the people that actually have the power to change your situation. Be creative with your approach and be persistent. If your specific counselor doesn't help you, go to another counselor, or another Rotarian that can talk to someone. Make friends with all the people in charge, because if you ever get caught in a dilemma that only your program can change (like changing host families) you want the people that have the power to change that to go out of their way to make your desires become a reality.

I saved the more specific tactics on how to win your family members over in Chapter 4. To learn those specific techniques and build stronger relationships with your host family look through Chapter 4. Strategies to make friends easier and quicker are the same strategies to get your host family to like you as well. They are universal laws that help anybody become more approachable and desirable to be around, whether it's around your friends or family members.

Summary:

- Always be polite and considerate to all members of your host family. Ask questions before doing things to make sure you aren't crossing any boundaries and to show you are putting their needs and feelings before yours.

- If your host family is rude and disrespectful towards you and you sense an actual problem with them, contact your exchange officers or whoever is in charge to help solve the problem.

- If you are absolutely stuck with a family you don't like and can't do anything about it, remember it's a learning process. You will come out a better person and will have gone through tremendous growth because of it.

My Experience:

I was blessed with two absolutely incredible host families for 5 months each and didn't have problems with any of them. There were many bumps in the road I had to figure out along the way in order to get on the same page, but nothing that ruined my experience as a whole. My first host family cared very much for me. They went out of their way to make sure I was always happy, had enough to eat, and was enjoying my stay with them. My host mom didn't speak any English but understood a little. My host dad spoke a little bit of English to where I could easily get away with just speaking English to him. My little brother who was around 12 years old didn't speak or understand any English.

I spent most of my time with my host mom since she was always home the same time I was. She was a very smart woman and actually taught Italian in school. So any time I had any question about definitions or grammar she would gladly help me. She held me to a very high standard and would always point out when I made silly mistakes speaking Italian. Getting corrected many times could easily bring down your confidence. Many other students would take this as an insult, but because I was determined to learn the language I knew it would help me learn it quicker so I encouraged her and everyone else to point out my mistakes. My first family was very strict on Rotary's rules however. I had a curfew and had to be home before midnight or I would be in trouble. Under their roof, I also could not drink or travel without having permission from Rotary. They kept a close eye on me and at times it got frustrating. Back home in America, my parents trusted me with anything. I was able to stay out as late as I wanted and sleep over a friend's house any time, so this was very new to me and took time adjusting too. This host family respected the Rotary rules with care and just wanted to make sure I was safe at all times, which I respect. I never broke the rules they had for me, and because of that, they trusted me. It's very important not to break their rules, because trust will make your life a whole lot easier with your family. If you do by any chance break the rules, because I know sometimes host parents may not understand and cooperate very well, it is very important you do not get caught. They can easily make your life hell. Respect their rules, and gain their trust, and you will find your life better and easier because of it. That's exactly what I did. I never came home late, and always asked their permission every time I went out with friends or did anything just so they weren't worried about me. Communication is key with your parents. Always communicate and trust will form as a result.

When looking for my second host family I had a bit of a problem however. It was one of the bigger problems I had all year. Pay close attention, because here is a great example of how I took control over something that had a drastic impact on how much I would enjoy the last few months on my exchange.

With my first host family, we were living near the city center so I always walked everywhere or rode my bike. In America it's not very common to walk or ride your bikes, but in Europe this mode of transportation may be the only way to get around for most exchange students like myself. Therefore, with my first host family, my living condition was very convenient. I could go anywhere easily with no problem.

For my second host family, they were going to move me outside the city in a secluded area with only one man that was never home because he worked all the time. He didn't have a bike for me, and if he did I wouldn't be able to use it because it was too far from the city. So, I would have to go with him to school an hour earlier in the morning because that's when he left for work and then take the bus back home every day. I was used to going home whenever I wanted because it was only a five-minute walk away. Therefore, I always stayed after class to talk to my friends, and hang out in the city center. Sometimes we would even get gelato or a bite to eat whenever we felt like it. I had a lot of freedom and I loved it that way. So, being tied down to a specific time schedule after experiencing that freedom that was not very appealing to me. And once I would go back home I would have to stay there unless I took another bus back to the center and back, which would be a huge inconvenience.

As you can imagine, after learning this was going to be my situation for the rest of my exchange, I was not very happy. I really did not want to live like this for the next 5 months so I started thinking and weighing out any possible options I had. After some time of thinking about it I had an idea. One of my closest friends who I had met from school just so happened to be an exchange student in New York the year before and so his family was very familiar with the Rotary exchange program. They were familiar with the rules, the process, and knew the exchange officers personally. I had met his parents one time, and they had heard about me from my friend many times before because we were very close.

So my idea was that I wondered if I could somehow get his family to host me as opposed to the other guy I was already assigned to. The chances were slim but I had to try. There was no reason not to. The more I thought about it, the more I realized it could be the perfect situation for me. His parents and I already knew of each other. Rotary already had an established relationship with this family. I could continue my extracurricular activities in the evening with no hassle. And other than living with one of my closest friends, the best part about it was that was he lived exactly in the middle of the city center. It was as good as it could possibly get in terms of location.

I called him one day and explained my whole situation to him. I told him I would greatly appreciate it if he could ask his parents if they could host me for the remainder of my exchange. I was a good kid and had a good reputation. Which is extremely important, especially in my small city because Italians talk a lot amongst themselves. If you messed up, everyone would know exactly what you did the next day. So, I hadn't caused any problems in the past which definitely helped. And after a night of thinking about it and talking it over after dinner, they called me actually agreed to host me. I was so freaking excited, I remember that moment so clearly.

HOWEVER, that was the easy part. Now I had to ask Rotary if it was ok and I had no idea what they would say because they had already planned on me going to live with the other guy. I stated my case and told them how this would negatively affect me and how I could benefit from staying with my friend. One major thing was I had basketball practice every evening at 8:30 p.m. and I couldn't just take a 30-minute bus ride to and from practice every night. Not only is it pretty dangerous, but it would waste too much time. I also just explained, how I wouldn't be experiencing the culture and everything being isolated by myself so far away from everyone else. And my friend's parents already said they would gladly host me, so finding another host family wasn't a problem.

As I said, I hadn't caused problems in the past so Rotary listened to me with a little more intent. My friend's mom even called Rotary and told them they agreed to it and tried to persuade them as well. After some organizing and figuring things out, the head exchange officer actually agreed to it. When I found out, I could not have been any happier. I went from almost being 30 minutes out all by myself to living with one of my best friends in the best location in town, for the remainder of my exchange. I basically took the worst possible scenario I could have had, and turned it to the best. His family was also very well off, so their house was very big and luxurious, which made my stay even more comfortable for me. Money and location aside, his family was extremely nice and caring to me which was the biggest thing in my eyes. They were super relaxed and chill. I got super close to my host parents and even saw them more so as friends than parents as time went by. I had no curfew and could basically do whatever I wanted as long as I didn't get in trouble. They would pour a glass of wine for me every dinner, and on the weekends when my host brother and I planned to go out to the city center he made sure my wine glass was always filled to the rim so I went out 'feeling good'. I lived like this for the next 5 months until my exchange ended. I was truly living my best life with them. I could not have imagined those few months with any other family. I would have been stuck in the other house, with one guy, had I not had the courage to try and change what I knew would be best for me.

This family was more lenient with the rules than my first one, mostly because they knew where I was coming from. Their son, my good friend, was my age and was a teenager looking to have fun just like me. He also did an exchange like me, so they knew exchange students just wanted to live their life and make the most of their exchange. In the end everything worked out, and because I was on both of my family's good side the whole time, I had a way better experience and could not have been any happier with my living arrangements.

Chapter 3: Learning the language

Learning the language of your host country could very well be the most difficult thing you learn to do while on your exchange. Many students go on exchange with absolutely zero experience in being able to speak their host countries language. Others go to countries where they have already learned the language beforehand. A good example of this is international students going on exchange to the States. Most students that go on exchange to English speaking countries already have a good grasp on the language. Some even know the language perfectly. But for those going to a country where they do not know the language, pay attention, because learning the language is very important to do.

If you truly want your experience to be the best it can be, learning your host countries language is an absolute must. And for those that already know their host country's language beforehand, I still encourage you to read through this chapter, because there is always room for improvement when learning a language. Especially when it comes to trying to perfect your accent to speak like a native.

Prior to leaving on your exchange you definitely need to study your host country's language. Your goal shouldn't be to try and learn the language perfectly, although if you can somehow pull that off beforehand, that would be the most ideal situation. Instead, this is to familiarize yourself with the language so you are not completely lost and confused when you arrive to the country. Noticing as little as one word while having your first conversation with your host family, will fire you up and you excite you. You will gain confidence and once you are in that "I can do this" mentality, then you are on the right path to learning the language.

So study the language before you leave. You can do this in multiple ways. Before we begin however, I'd just like to preface by saying I know you've probably heard some of these methods before, but I'm listing them anyway because I've either 1.) Used them personally or 2.) Seen them work through others, and know you can still take away something you might not have thought of before.

1. Rosetta Stone

Let's say you have absolutely no clue how to speak a language. For example, you don't even know how to say one world, I highly suggest starting off with Rosetta Stone. This is because Rosetta Stone moves at a very slow pace and is great at familiarizing the user with the very basic essential words. The difficulty gradually increases as you practice more and more, but it's very consistent with making sure you get the foundation of the language correct before you move on. If you have absolutely no idea how to speak the language this may be the best option for you. However, if you do choose Rosetta Stone, keep in mind that it will require more of your time for practice. Meaning that you should start this a few months in advance before going on your exchange. The other major negative to using Rosetta Stone is that it one of the more expensive options. It can cost up to $300 depending on the package, and for most that is a deal breaker. However, as students, you might have access to free Rosetta Stone through your educational institution. Many large university's for example offer this included in their tuition. Luckily there are many other effective resources available that are free to use.

2. Apps: Duo Lingo

Another resource I recommend using is Duo Lingo. Duo Lingo is an app designed specifically for learning a new language, and there are many others like it, but I believe this one works best for the average exchange student learning a new language. I downloaded many apps and I found this one to be my favorite. Just like Rosetta Stone it starts off with the basics and gradually increases difficulty as you progress through the app. There are a few reasons why I love this app so much. First of all, it's completely free and very simple to use. You set up a profile, set your target language, and select weekly goals. You set daily goals of how long you wish to learn the language every day and the app even keeps you accountable by sending you daily emails to remind you to knock out that daily goal for every day you don't log in. It's also very fun to use because it is set up like a game where you need to complete one module to move onto the next and are rewarded achievement and gems by completing certain modules. Modules are the different topics of a language to learn like basics, greetings, foods, animals, places, etc. It even tracks your skill level for all module and therefore tracks what part of the language you are best and weakest at. It then gives you the option to 'practice weak skills' so you are constantly improving areas that you need more focus on. Definitely try out this app if you get the chance. I used it not only before my exchange, but throughout my whole exchange as well and even afterwards to make sure I didn't forget the language.

3. Movies

One other thing you can do is to watch movies in the language you are trying to learn. This is a great idea because you can learn the language while simultaneously enjoying yourself and being relaxed in bed or somewhere cozy. I recommend watching it in your host country's language with subtitles from your own language. This is beneficial because one of the positives of learning a language through watching movies is that you get to listen and learn the accent as well. With Rosetta Stone and Duo Lingo you can learn what to say pretty well, but you can't learn how to say things very well compared to when you are actually listening to natives speak in conversation with each other. When watching movies however, you can switch it up as well. Sometimes I would have the movie in Italian with English subtitles. Other times I would even have it in English with Italian Subtitles so I can read the Italian words down below and match it to the action they were doing on screen. Keep in mind however, words aren't translated word for word between languages, so you will have a difficult time trying to match up the subtitles with what they are saying in your native language. Other times when I would watch movies, I would even just have it in Italian with Italian subtitles. This was not to understand the movie, because I wasn't going to understand the whole movie this way. But it helped a lot in hearing other people speak the language and following what they were saying through the subtitles to see how the words were pronounced and the flow of the sentence structure as well. All this was to just familiarize myself with the language- how it flows- and to see how natives pronounced certain words while trying to figure out the plot through context clues. Watching movies is just another method of learning the language that I recommend every exchange student incorporate on your personal journey to fluency.

4. Books

I would also recommend buying books on learning a language. I have bought workbooks similar to what you would find in a classroom and I have also bought mini books you can find in bookstores that contain the basics of each category in a language. For example, simple phrases to know what to say when you greet someone, when talking about food, work, hobbies, sports etc... Everything you need in order to have a basic conversation. The best kinds of books to read however, are children's books. I strongly recommend getting some children's books with images and reading those. They are designed to help children learn the language, so they can definitely help you as well.

5. Songs

Another fun way to learn the language is downloading songs and playing them on repeat. It is a bonus if you can find a song you actually like, because then it is easier to just listen to it all the time. It will actually make you interested in learning the words. Search up online, the best songs in that foreign language and download each one you see. Then when you're walking to class, chilling in your room or driving around, play them and try to listen to the words. This allows you to be learning while also multitasking on something else that requires little attention and focus. It makes learning a language so much more enjoyable and is what many students around the world do to learn a language. And who knows maybe if you're out with your friends and that song comes on you will actually know the lyrics to it and will be able to dance along.

6. Sticky notes

Sticky notes are another popular way to learn many useful words in your host language. Simply write the word of the object on a sticky note in your host language and stick them to all associated objects around your room. You will learn all the objects you create sticky notes for very quickly, because you will see the words around you every day. This is a great way to learn the vocabulary of everyday objects that surround you.

7. Change the Language on your Phone

Something else I did that really helped me, was I switched my phone to Italian instead of English. It was really frustrating at first because I couldn't navigate around my phone well especially when I was in the 'Settings', but it forced me to learn. I learned the months, days of the week, and many other Italian words that would pop up on my screen. After a while you get used to it, and it definitely helps with getting you more familiar with the language.

These are all different things you can do to start learning a language. Keep in mind, these tactics are not only limited to before you leave. Each one of these strategies you can also implement while you are on your exchange or even after so you are constantly learning and not forgetting what you have learned.

Now, let's discuss different ways you can learn the language once you arrive in your host country.

As I just mentioned, keep doing all these things once you arrive. You will begin to learn everything a lot quicker because you will recognize everything you have already studied before. And although these different tactics I just mentioned are great ways of learning the language they don't even compare to how much more quicker you can learn a language using this next tactic.

I cannot stress this enough, if you really want to learn a language inside and out, it is absolutely imperative that you put yourself in a situation that forces you to speak the language. So what do I mean by this?

I mean you have to be constantly surrounded by people of your native country. This starts with your host family. If your host family is speaking to you in your native tongue, you are in deep trouble. I know how frustrating it is, to not be able to communicate with your family and friends because you don't know the language. Therefore, you resort to speaking your native language if that is an option for you, but you are setting yourself up for failure if you do this. If you really want to learn a new language, you have to be willing to get out your comfort zone. It sucks in the beginning, I know. But what I also do know, is your future self will thank you. So demand your family to only speak to you in the language you are trying to learn. They will respect you for it, and if they have a problem with it because it is too frustrating for them as well, contact your counselor or supervisor to demand a switch of families or talk to them about it to try and fix the situation. If your host family doesn't know your native language, and you're forced to speak their language, you are on the right path. It is very frustrating at first, but in the future, looking back on it, you will prefer it that way because it's what allowed you to learn the language the quickest way.

All this happens in the household, but it also has to continue outside the household with your friends. Now, listen to me. You HAVE to make friends FROM YOUR HOST COUNTRY.

(If you're struggling with making friends in your host country, don't worry I talk about it in the next chapter. But for now, let's assume you are able to make friends with the people from your host country with no problem.)

First off, I know exchange students are the best friends you are ever going to make in your life, but there is a huge problem with this. Most exchange students only speak to each other in English. And if you're in an English speaking country that's ok. But if you're not, this is a big problem. In the beginning of the year, when no one really knows the language, it's ok to speak to each other in English or whatever other language you guys are familiar with. But try to transition over to your host country's language as time goes on and both of you become more fluent. Similarly, exchange students from the same country speak to each other in their native language and not their host language; this could also be a very big problem. It keeps you from learning the language you need to know, and it also excludes the other exchange students from engaging with you in your conversation which could potentially danger your relationship with the other exchange students. You might not think it's a big deal because the other exchange students aren't involved in the conversation, but trust me it can still be very annoying to them.

Exchange students are great friends to have, but making friends with the natives is just as important if not more important. Yes I know, exchange students just understand each other at level no one else can. Everyone is on the same boat, on the same journey, going through the same obstacles, and experiencing the same thing, so it makes everyone become best friends. And that's ok. I am not saying not to make friends with exchange students. What I am saying is you also have to make friends from school, sports, organizations, or any other way so they can speak to you in their language. If you have already made friends, make sure they speak to you in their native language, but even just by being surrounded by natives, you pick up on a lot of other things. The way they speak, different words used in different contexts, and even more importantly, the slang. Learning the slang is a good way to immerse yourself in the culture and gain respect from your fellow peers and family members. Learning the language isn't about sounding like a robot. The whole point of learning a language is to connect with other people. Learning the language gives you that deeper connection with someone else, and if you speak to them like a person and not like you're taking a test, it is easier to make that connection. So surround yourself with other people, and even if you can't speak the language listen closely, and try to pay attention. The same words, phrases, and slang you hear from everyone will start sounding very familiar and before you know it, you will start saying them as well.

And even if you don't understand something ask questions. Whether it's to your friends, your teachers, or your family. Asking questions in one of the best things you can do to learn the language. This does multiple things:

It clarifies things to help you understand conversations better. Maybe you didn't know one word in a sentence, and asking what it means clarifies what the other person was trying to say and now you understand the sentence as a whole just because of that one word.

It helps you remember. You are asking a question and that sometimes leads to a little conversation about the word or phrase you are asking about. Therefore you are spending time on it and further encoding it into your memory.

Others will see you are actively trying to learn the language. This is incredibly important. If the natives recognize you trying to learn their own language you will gain respect from them. They will like you more, and they will be more willing to help you. When someone sees you taking the time to learn their language and culture as well for example, they are more willing to help you succeed. They will go out of their way to help you learn, because they see it is very important to you, and won't see it as a waste of their time.

Trust me you don't want to be that kid that's left out of the conversation and all the fun because you don't understand what is going on. Don't be dead weight to your friends and family. They sacrifice so much for you, the least you can do is try to connect with them in their own language. You will make more memories and have a better experience because you will actually feel included. And not only that, it makes life a whole lot easier. You are not limited to daily functions. You can go out and have fun and not worry about meeting new people. When you meet new people and speak to them in their language, I promise you they will be very impressed and you will feel really good about yourself.

Once you have gained a basic understanding of the language, and can somewhat keep a conversation going, don't be afraid of making mistakes while you speak. I can't stress this enough! DO NOT BE AFRAID TO FAIL. Speak and if someone, corrects you, GOOD. You just learned what you didn't know before. You want people to correct you. Don't forget that. You want to tell everyone you know to correct you. It will suck in the beginning because you will feel like you absolutely suck at speaking the language, but you are learning a new language for crying out loud. That is extremely difficult to do, cut yourself some slack. Tell your friends and family to correct you, and once they start doing that, you begin to learn at an exponential rate. You tend to not make the same mistakes before, and change what you thought might have been correct, to what actually is correct. Sometimes people feel bad for correcting you because they don't want to bring you down or discourage you, but you need to tell them to do so anyway. If you keep the old habits of incorrect grammar, it will only be harder to change once you start learning the language more. It's also very annoying to other people you talk to if you're constantly making the same little grammatical mistakes. If you keep saying something that is clearly wrong every time, but you don't even notice it is wrong which is why you keep saying it, it could be really irritating to others you spend a lot of time with.

And if someone does correct you, don't take it personal! You might feel someone is criticizing you, especially if you are not close to the person, but most of the time they are not. They want what is best for you, and you should be grateful they are saying something. It means you are learning. And if they are actually criticizing you then who cares. You don't want to be surrounded by people that bring you down in the first place. You want to be surrounded by positive people that make you a better person and only give you constructive criticism. Who cares what the others think, they aren't the ones living in another country, living the best life they could possibly imagine for themselves.

Additionally, if you are on a yearlong exchange, it is also important to note the stages and time frame it typically takes someone from knowing nothing about a language to become fluent in one for the average student that goes on exchange. I have created a timeline of where you should be after a certain amount of months to guide you to where exactly you need to be to learn the language. Think of each of the following timelines as a checkpoint or goal. Once you arrive at that checkpoint, you should be where the description describes you in terms of how well you know the language. If you are behind and realize you have no reason to be, considering your circumstances compared to others, then you need to pick up the pace. If the description describes where exactly you are at in terms of how well you are learning the language then you are on the right track. This is strictly based on what I observed through my experience however, and tends to be correct for the exchange students that actively try to learn the language.

But keep in mind this for the average exchange student that is actively trying to learn the new language. You may be further ahead of the timeline, which is good, it just all depends on different variables like how much easier learning a language comes to you, what language you are learning, how much time you put into studying the language, the group of people you hang out with, your family, and all the other factors that play a role in determining how you can learn a language.

Beginning:

Here you know nothing. You don't know how to keep a conversation with someone. You might have learned words and phrases that mean something, but you never actually use them in conversation. You have no idea what anyone is telling you when they speak in their own language and that's ok.

Month 3:

Anywhere around 3rd month, this is when the typical exchange student actually understands the everyday conversation of the spoken language. You begin to understand what people are telling you, not 100% of everything, but you are able to piece things together and use context clues to understand basic - intermediate conversation. You still can't speak yet. You might reply in your native language if you're an English speaker, or you might just reply with the same basic phrases and words you have come to learn that can be used for various situations. But speaking in full sentences still is a huge problem, which is ok.

Months 3-5:

For many of you, this will be a very frustrating time period. This is the period where you understand a lot of what people are saying to you, but for the life of you, you can't respond back. You feel like you know the language a little bit because you can engage in a conversation by listening and understanding when people are talking, but when it's your turn to speak you just can't find the words or complete the sentence. This is ok, it is simply a plateau in the learning curve of the language. Once you get over this hump, you will feel a lot more relieved, and less frustrated even though you still won't speak with complete fluency. This period is essentially the transition from not speaking at all to being able to actually speak a little bit.

Month 5:

By now you should be able to speak a little bit and hold a basic conversation with someone you just met. There will for sure be things you do not know or understand when people ask you, but you should be able to get around, still rather uncomfortably. It's easier to learn more of the language from this point, because you have previous knowledge of the language that you can piece together and use as a foundation. The graph to which learning a language can most similarly be compared to is the exponential graph. At this point, you are starting to rise and learn more in a quicker way. The whole beginning just seemed like you were getting nowhere, but after you beat that hump, it starts getting a lot easier from here. You may also first experience dreaming in your host language around this time period. When you do first dream in your host language you should be proud, it is a huge accomplishment and a sign that the language is getting engraved into your subconscious mind.

Month 7:

By now you have had two months to learn even more on speaking. You understand the vast majority, but you are still learning on understanding the language of course as you will most likely never understand everything from the language, just huge amounts at best. But in terms of speaking, you can now speak to your friends and family for sure with conversations at a time using few English (or your native language) words to get your point across. Your grammar may still suck, that's ok, because you are able to communicate a lot more effortlessly.

Month 8:

You are still learning at an exponential rate, so your conversation skills are a lot more fluid and things start coming out of your mouth a lot more subconsciously. You should also be dreaming more in your host language because it is starting to get a lot more engraved in your subconscious mind. By now you should only be talking to your friends and family in your native language. You are still obviously making many errors and mistakes, but you get your point across and can hang out with your friends and family only speaking that language. At this point, you may also be incorporating slang a lot more in your daily language.

Months 9 & 10:

You should be considered fluent by this point. Again, you still may make many errors and mistakes, but that is supposed to happen. You conjugate words very well in all tenses and can understand almost anything, especially using context clues. You have no problem, making a reservation online, or going to buy a new sim card for your phone. You can get around just by yourself, and you feel very confident in the language. By now you are also getting better at your accent. Accent plays a huge role in the language and should be taken into consideration throughout the whole process of learning the language. Only once you can speak the language very well can you turn your primary focus to getting better at your accent. Your accent is the true determination of how well you can speak a language from the perspective of a native person. But get the basics down first, and focus on actually being able to speak the language before you prioritize your accent. You are still not perfect at speaking the language however, but you have come a very long way and you should be able to now truly consider yourself fluent in that language. You should be able to put on a resume that you know this language, to where even if an employer interviewed you in this language you'd be able to cruise through the interview. Again, your vocabulary and grammar may not be perfect, but for example, for an English speaker speaking German, Portuguese, or whatever it is, everyone will be very impressed and consider you completely fluent.

Summary:

- Study your host language before you leave on your exchange with the different strategies listed. The goal isn't to become fluent in the language, but to familiarize yourself with it so you don't become overwhelmed.

- No amount of studying the language on your own will ever top how much you can learn by just surrounding yourself with native people from your host country who are constantly speaking to you in their language.

- Do not be afraid to fail when speaking! Practice and put yourself out there. You want people to correct you, it means you're getting rid of the old habits and replacing them with new ones.

My experience:

I came out of my exchange year being completely fluent in Italian. However, I already knew a little bit of Spanish. I wasn't completely fluent, but I understood quite a bit and spoke at a basic conversation level. Although I only knew the basics of Spanish it sure did help a lot. Italian and Spanish are two very different languages, but they both derive from Latin which makes them very similar in structure, format, and accent as well. Therefore, it was definitely easier for me to comprehend Italian over time compared to other students, especially through reading rather than listening. When I first arrived in Italy, I understood absolutely nothing that was being communicated to me, even with my Spanish background. My Spanish helped when learning conjugations and learning certain vocabulary, but I didn't have a huge advantage because I wasn't completely fluent in it. For those fluent Latin language speakers, you will find it way easier to pick up another Latin Language, even if you understand completely nothing in the beginning. The conjugations and certain vocabulary are very similar to each other. The flow of the sentences and structure will be nothing out of the ordinary for you as well.

But anyways, before I left to Italy, I was dumb and did not study the language at all. Right before I left to Italy I thought 'Ciao' was French. I had bought a couple of books to study, watched a couple of movies in Italian, and downloaded Duo Lingo, but by the time I did all those things it was already too late. I started preparing for the language about a week or two before my exchange which was not nearly enough time. Once I started realizing that I was actually pretty screwed and hadn't learned anything I started feeling anxious and nervous. I didn't know anything about the language and I didn't do anything far in advance enough to learn it.

I remember meeting my host family at the airport and on the ride home they were speaking in Italian to each other the whole time. All I can remember on that car ride back was just thinking, "Oh. My. God. I am so screwed..." I didn't understand anything. Not one word; and it all just seemed like gibberish. I couldn't even differentiate the words from each other and point out the pauses in the sentences. It all just seemed like a flow of nonsense.

My host dad had an intermediate speaking level of English, so I was able to communicate with him in English if I wanted to. My host mother did not know any English at all. It was strictly Italian with her, which was scary to find out. My little host brother was the same, he did not know any English at all. And my host sister who was only there temporarily before she left back to University in Venice in a couple of weeks, spoke perfect English. So I communicated through her and my dad most of the time. When I was with my mom, we would only use body language, google translate, and even point at stuff we were talking about. However, they all spoke in just Italian to each other. For example, at the dinner table they would converse in only Italian and I was just there trying to figure out exactly what was going on. They only spoke English to me the first few days and even weeks when they were actually trying to get to know me. This is ok, because you are going to be with this family for a few months, and you need to build early rapport somehow.

Therefore, after the first few days of being at home with my sister and dad as English speakers at the house, I wasn't totally uncomfortable and scared. About 3 days after I arrived, the best friend of the girl I exchanged families with who was now in Texas, texted me and wanted to hang out. I was so grateful to have this girl,

Francesca, reach out to me and invite me to hang out with her and her friends. We were texting in English and we arranged for her to come pick me up, so she could walk me over to the city center and hang out with her and her friends. We had nice long conversations texting each other, getting to know each other and making plans. When she arrived at my place I formally introduced myself again and began telling her how thankful I was to have her reach out to me. She then looked at me with a blank stare and said, "No no, non parlo Inglese.." I then preceded to find out she couldn't speak any English. She had been using Google Translate to communicate with me the whole time. So the entire 10 min walk to the center was us typing what we wanted to say to each other on google translate. As you can imagine, it was very awkward. When we arrived with the rest of the group I found out they didn't speak English very well either, but it was enough to barely get to know each other and hang out. They were embarrassed to speak English, like most Italians are, but we managed and they were incredibly kind to me. I had one of the most fun days on my exchange that day. Even though we couldn't completely communicate with each other, they showed me around the city, gave me a tour of the city cathedral, took me to get a glass of wine, took me to another place to get food and gelato, and they paid for everything! They even took me up the Torrazzo, which was the bell tower next to the cathedral that overlooked the whole city. It's one of the largest bell towers in all of Europe which had a magnificent view overlooking the city and landscape. Anyways, I had an absolutely incredible day. Other than not communicating to the best of our abilities, it couldn't have been any better. Language was definitely a huge barrier, but we communicated more through body language and emotion and that's how we became very close. They ended up becoming some of my closest friends on my entire exchange.

After that long fun day, we all decided to get a shot of espresso at a nearby coffee shop before we headed back home (because that's just what Italians do). This coffee shop had a nice view of the Cathedral and bell tower and was located at the base of a building about a thousand years old. I couldn't wrap my head around the fact that this was now my home. While I was sitting there enjoying my coffee I realized, I really like these people. Not in a superficial friendship kind-of-way, but in a deep way. I really enjoyed hanging out with them and being around them. They made me very happy and I wanted them to be my best friends.

While I was contemplating all that however, I look over at them and have an epiphany. I see all 5 of them enjoying their coffee, laughing hysterically, enjoying the moment, and having a great time... while speaking Italian to each other. I did not understand one word that was coming out of their mouth. You can tell how much fun they were having just based off their body language, all the laughter, and tone in which they spoke. And I felt left out. They continued all that for about 30 minutes. They tried to engage me as much as they could, but they were so caught up in their conversation that I felt left out. And who's to blame them, it's not their fault I don't know the language of the country I'm now currently living in. So, for almost 30 minutes I was so frustrated with myself. That whole day was like a tease. It showed me what I could be a part of if I learned the language and was actually able to connect with amazing people like them. I was pissed at myself. I felt like I was missing out and it was completely my fault. I by no means expected them to go out of their way to speak English to me. I didn't to be the dead-weight that people carry around. I didn't like feeling like a crutch that people always had to care for. I just remember having this awful feeling in my stomach that reminded me that this whole thing was now my reality. I felt helpless, unwanted, and miserable. I was missing out on an opportunity to become best friends with some amazing people, and I couldn't understand anything they were saying. I couldn't relate at all, and I just felt like I was in the background. I knew if I didn't learn the language I would just continue to be put in the background for the rest of the year. I never wanted to feel like this again. I never wanted to feel like I wasn't a part of a group solely because I didn't take it upon myself to learn the language. So just like I had learned about in all the self-help books I had previously read, and just like I explained to you in chapter one, on how to tackle these situations with the proper mindset, I got pissed and studied my ass off to learn the language. If I didn't learn the language I knew it was going to be COMPLETELY my fault and no one else's.

Therefore, I took it upon myself to learn.

I paid attention to every single thing someone was saying, even if I didn't understand. I would try to look for patterns and words I had heard before.

I studied all the little books I bought to learn the language. I would memorize and write down the phrases that I knew I would use the most and tried to implement them when was talking to people.

I downloaded Duo Lingo and spent at least 30 minutes on it every single day. I had other apps to help me learn the language, but this was the one I consistently stuck to because I personally liked it the most.

I watched movies in Italian with Italian subtitles. The reason I would watch movies in Italian with Italian subtitles was not to try and understand and actually enjoy the movie, but to learn how each word sounded from an actual Italian voice. It helped me familiarize myself with the Italian accent and see how certain words were spelled and pronounced. I would constantly stop and rewind the movie to understand exactly what the actors were saying and how they were saying it with their accent.

I always asked questions. When I didn't know something I always asked, and my Italian friends and family would go above and beyond to try and help me understand the concept. They would even take out paper and start drawing and writing different ways to help me understand the concept. They saw how committed I was and they saw my progress which encouraged them to help me more.

I told everyone I knew to speak to me in Italian. I could not speak Italian AT ALL for the first couple of months. But I still told them to speak to me in Italian, and I would at least respond in English, if I couldn't in Italian (which was almost all the time in the beginning). It helped that, in the city I was in, many people did not speak English. They all studied English their whole lives, but were too embarrassed to actually speak it to a native English speaker. So almost everybody I met already spoke to me in mainly Italian, with few English words, which was perfect for me.

I studied the language every day in school. I got lucky because I didn't have to take any classes. I had to stay in class every day and listen, but I wasn't being graded for a couple of reasons: 1.) I told them I didn't know the language at all so I physically and mentally couldn't do any of the work the teachers were handing out to the rest of the class and 2.) I had already graduated from high school in America so grades didn't matter to me. I explained to the teachers I had already graduated and I needed to just learn the language for now before doing things like physics and math that I already

47

knew. I even went out of my way to ask my Italian teacher to print out basic worksheets for me to learn the language and she did. The teachers don't want to see you doing nothing, so she went out of her way to make worksheets that I could practice to help me study. But what really helped me, was the fact that since I wasn't really studying in school I had 5 hours every day Monday - Saturday in a classroom of doing absolutely nothing. So when I wasn't in another classroom visiting or teaching English I got this huge spiral notebook and wrote anything and everything down that could help me learn Italian. I started by writing all verbs I could find and separating them into the categories of -ire, -ere, and -are ending verbs. I would then write the definition of each one next to it so I knew what it meant. Then, I would have another few pages of all tenses of the verb (past-tense, present-tense, future-tense, perfect past, imperfect pass, etc.) on the notebook and conjugated them according to each tense so I could know which way to use that verb when I was speaking in that tense. I did this for all the verbs - the word, with the definition, and all the conjugations.

I would also write down many pages of just phrases I knew I would need. For example, any simple greeting I knew I would use dealing with food, studying, etiquette, sports, etc. Literally anything I knew I would need to know I wrote it down. I even wrote a full front and back page of all the bad words in the language. Those were actually the first words I learned because all your friends are always so eager to teach you the bad words first. And quite honestly they are very important to learn. It's part of the slang that connects you with your friends and peers. They will find it hilarious if they hear you curse in their language. Don't curse all the time however, especially in front of adults, kids, or your host family. Just when you are around your friends in a controlled manner. No one likes someone who curses too much. Anyways, I wrote down everything I needed to learn, and committed it to memory so

I can start practicing it all in conversation. I did this for the first couple of months while stuck in the classroom, and my Italian became very good, very fast. You might not have 5 hours Monday - Saturday like I did. Not everyone's exchange is the same. You have to the best with what you're given. It's up to you and not anyone else.

Even after all those hours of studying and memorizing by myself, I would still argue what helped me the most was probably that I had many Italian friends. Being surrounded by people speaking the language and making an effort to pay attention to them will work wonders. I hung out constantly with my Italian friends and they always went out of their way to help me learn. I had this one friend in my class, who I considered one of my best friends while I was on exchange, Francesco Antoldi. He went out of his way to make sure I learned the language, and would always call me out when he saw me speaking English. He was extremely patient with me literally all year, and I owe the majority of my Italian speaking skills to that man right there. In exchange, I even taught him a little bit of English, and English slang as well. It was a relationship, where we were both learning and gaining something from each other. These are the longest lasting, highest quality kind of friendships. The ones where you are both learning and benefitting from each other. Find someone like Francesco Antoldi, someone who keeps you accountable.

Those are all the ways I personally learned the language on my exchange. I was ahead of the time frame I laid out for you earlier in the chapter but I grinded hard, and I know you can too. Throughout the whole year, I was constantly being given compliments on how good my Italian was. Almost everybody I met was amazed by how much I had learned after I told them I knew nothing when I arrived. I'm not trying to brag by any means, I'm just here to show you that's it's possible and that the rewards will definitely follow the hard work. Everyone was impressed by me and the progress I made. After about 6 months I only spoke to people in Italian with a few things in English I did not yet know of course, but I challenged myself to only speak to everyone I knew in Italian and even texted only in Italian. I messed up a lot as well, I mean A LOT. I messed up almost every time I attempted to speak, but I really did not care at all, because I had the mentality that it was better to mess up in the language I was trying to learn, than not mess up in the language I already knew. And I was right. It paid off tenfold. It gave people the opportunity to correct me and once they corrected me, I would not make that same error again in the future.

The exchange student group that lived in the same city as me, had the same mentality as well. Even though we were all on completely different levels on where we were at in learning the language, we decided to only speak to ourselves in Italian, and it actually worked. For the whole second half of the exchange, when we all had a basic understanding of how to speak, we would only speak to each other in Italian. We had students from Mexico and Brazil that spoke almost perfect Italian so early in the year that it was not a problem for them to speak to us in Italian. I learned from them as well. I was humble enough to always ask for help with anything I needed, even from the exchange students, and never saw it as a competition between them to see who could learn the language the fastest. We were all on the same boat, and we all tried helping each other to improve and become better. If you can get your exchange group to speak the native language, then that would help you learn the language a lot quicker as well.

I ended up learning the language really well, and when I came back to the U.S. I knew I was screwed because no one there spoke Italian. So I continued studying and using Duo Lingo as much as I could. I kept in touch with my friends and host families by speaking only in Italian still, which helped me retain a lot of what I learned abroad as well. I came back to the States, started college at Texas A&M University and the first week I decided to take the Italian Placement Exam to see how well I actually knew the language. I didn't necessarily do it for the credits I would have received if I scored well, only to see how much I actually thought I knew. I ended up taking the test, and got an almost perfect score. I got a lot of Italian credit, and now I have a minor in Italian. Which is pretty cool to talk about when it comes up in a conversation.

Chapter 4: Making friends quickly and easily

Making friends on exchange can be a real problem for many people. You are the new guy/girl in town and know absolutely no one, and to make it worse you might not even know the language. This is very scary for many people and rightfully so. We try very hard to make friends and get people to like us, and some friendships come naturally and easily throughout your exchange, but many others do not.

If you want to make more friends, you are simply going to have to put yourself in situations where you can meet more people. You can do this by always going out and doing things either with your host family or current people you know. You can also get involved in the community or organizations in school. Join clubs or sports and constantly be trying to put yourself where people naturally get to know each other. You can also leverage the people you currently know, into meeting the people they know. Then once you become friends with those new people, you leverage their network as well and so on. The most difficult way to meet new people for some exchange students, but the most effective and time efficient is to straight up go introduce yourself to people. This could be anybody in your class, a new friend group your around, or anyone in the city. Anytime anywhere, you can always go up and meet new people. You even have the topic of you being an exchange student as a conversation starter with anyone you begin talking to.

Simply put yourself in situations where you will naturally meet more people. Get out of your comfort zone and begin speaking with someone you don't know. This is definitely easier said than done. Many people get really anxious and are afraid of the fear of rejection and humiliation. You must try your absolute best to overcome this fear. If you do, you have an insane advantage over many exchange students worldwide.

The bigger problem I see with exchange students on their exchange is not meeting new people. Anyone can go up and introduce themselves to someone if they really wanted, and anyone can get involved and constantly put themselves in situations where they are meeting new people. The problem I've seen in the past, is creating friendships or lasting relationships through the people you have already briefly met.

You want people to come back and talk to you again after you have met them. Well, how do you do this? It's important to understand that every relationship begins with a first impression. You need to try and get people to instantly like you based off their first impression of you and first conversation with you. Not many people know how to do this. It's hard because many natives are already content with the friends they have and may convince themselves they already have enough friends. However, the fact that you are a foreign exchange student puts you at an advantage. First of all, people will most likely already know you are an exchange student and therefore know you are not from around there. This will make people already know a little bit about you which will make them more comfortable to come up and talk to you since they know what to start the conversation with. Some might even have sympathy realizing you probably don't know anyone and will come up and talk to you without having to do anything yourself. But for the people that don't want to go out of their way to make new friends, you may have still grabbed their interest without you even knowing. That is because, even though they may already be content with the group of friends they already have, you provide something different. You are an exchange student from a different part of the world, with a different background, beliefs, ideas, and culture. You can provide value to someone else's life just by being from somewhere else, which makes you uniquely different.

This will automatically grab many people's attention, however it won't guarantee friendships. It won't guarantee they will come up to you and force themselves on you to be their friend. To ensure they will want to come back to you again and be your friend you must leave them with a great lasting impression of you. I mentioned a few of these briefly earlier in the first chapter, but here are a few very powerful techniques you can apply, that will make you instantly more approachable and well-liked by the people you meet.

1. Remembering people's names

I can't stress how important it is to remember people's names. Dale Carnegie in his book *How to Win Friends and Influence People*, says the sweetest and most important sound to anybody in any language is hearing their own name. This is such a powerful tool when trying to get people to like you. There were many times where I met someone and only talked to them for 5 minutes and remembered their name. Then when we saw each other again a couple weeks later I would say, "Hi (whatever their name is)". They would always be completely shocked that I was able to remember their name. If you put in the effort to remember someone else's name it makes them feel special. It will make them feel more important and will automatically get them like you more. This accomplishes two things: First, they will want to be around you more because you give them that sense of importance which is a good feeling for everyone. Not everyone gives people that feeling, and thus they will be more drawn to hanging out with you. Second, it makes them feel bad for not knowing your name back. If you call someone by their name and you guys have met before, they will instantly feel guilty because they noticed you remembered their name and they don't remember yours. Then, they will go through extra effort to remember your name, and this leads to a closer relationship between you and that person.

2. Be enthusiastic and radiate positive energy

It's no secret that people are subconsciously attracted and drawn to those that are more optimistic and enthusiastic about life. We have all met these people, where anytime we are in their presence we just feel good about ourselves, and we want to hang around them more. You must express emotion of enthusiasm and positivity whenever you meet someone new. These emotions are contagious and people will naturally be drawn to you. Everybody wants these kinds of people in their lives. When you meet someone and show how excited and grateful you are to be in their wonderful country, they will like you way more and will find a way to hang out with you whenever they can. This is especially true for the adults you meet. Nothing makes an adult happier than seeing someone from a different country enjoy life and express signs of happiness in their home country. Change your tone of voice and greet people with excitement when you first meet them. By showing them how happy you are by getting to meet them I guarantee they will be thinking, "dang I really like this person".

Don't forget to smile as well. Always smile. Dale Carnegie also said in his book "The expression one wears on one's face is far more important than the clothes one wears on one's back". It shows you are a happy soul and will make you more approachable. People are way more likely to approach the smiling happy fellow as opposed to the person who looks grouchy or gloomy. In my experience, I noticed the exchange students that were way most liked were the people that always smiled and were always enthusiastic. It really is contagious and is extremely powerful. If you can learn to greet people like this I promise, they will find you more friendly and approachable. You leave that person with a lasting positive impression about you. What you say is not as important as how you say it. People remember not what you said but how you made them feel. Therefore, next time they see you they will be happy to see you and more inclined to go up and talk to you. It's all body language, which is specifically more important if you can't speak the language very well. Learn to do this, and you will make more friends quickly.

3. Become genuinely interested in the other person

Dale Carnegie also mentioned in his book, "You can make more friends in 2 months by becoming interested in other people than you can in 2 years by trying to get other people interested in you." It doesn't matter who you are, all of us like people who admire us. When someone shows interest in you it makes you feel important. And like I said earlier, we all like to feel like we're important. John Dewey, famous American philosopher said, "The deepest urge in human nature is the desire to feel important". If you commit this quote to memory and apply it with everyone you come in contact with, people will instantly like you. We all want to be around people that show interest in us. Therefore, if you show interest in someone else, whether it be their hobbies, background, stories, or past experiences and get them to talk about all those things they love to talk about, they will love hanging around you. The goal in any conversation you have with people you are meeting on your exchange is to show interest in them, and not to try and get them to become interested in you. It has to be genuine and sincere interest. People will know when you are faking it. The only time it is acceptable to try and get them a little interested in you is in the beginning of the relationship with the person when they are trying to learn all about you, your culture, and previous experiences back home. Talk about yourself and answer any questions they may have but don't overdo it. Many people just ask questions to keep the conversation going. Train yourself to spot the difference when people are asking you questions to continue the conversation or because they are actually interested in what you have to say. Ultimately, you should get them talking more about themselves than you about yourself. Learn this and apply it and you will be amazed at where it takes you.

4. Show that you are genuinely interested in the country's culture, language, and tradition.

Aside from showing interest in the individual when you are talking to them, also show interest in their country and its culture, language, and traditions. People have a strong emotional connection with their own country. If you show them that you are trying your best to integrate and familiarize yourself well with their country, they will see that you care. By complementing the country and culture you are indirectly complimenting the person you are talking to, because that's part of their identity and who they are. They embody their country and everything having to do with it. Many people take pride in where they live and the traditions they grew up with. So if you show that you are genuinely interested in getting to know about the country, they will be flattered. They see that you came to learn and grow and aren't just here to have fun. They will appreciate your effort in trying to learn more about everything. Always try and ask questions about the country's history, traditions, food, political system, etc. People will be more than happy to help you learn about them. If you show curiosity followed by appreciation, they will see this as a huge compliment. You don't always have to agree with the way that country does things, but if you show appreciation and compliment them about what you do really like about it they will like you more for it. People like people who are like them. Find similar interests that you have with someone else and talk about them. Most people love their country, and if they don't, they most certainly love some of the traditions and cultural aspects about it. By finding something about their country that you both like, you can build a great relationship with someone just by talking about it.

5. Encourage others to talk about themselves

This point goes hand in hand with point number three. People love to talk about themselves. People's favorite subject is themselves. If you get people to talk about themselves they will always want to talk to you. It's just like every other tactic. It makes them feel good and makes them want to be around you more. Ask them about their hobbies and what they like to do in their free time. Ask about their beliefs and opinions on certain things. Encourage them to talk about their past accomplishments.

This will make them feel important and good about themselves, and want to remain friends with you.

By getting others to talk about themselves, you are also learning a lot about them, which you can use to your advantage in getting closer to them. You might find you have similar interests or you can use something they mentioned as a conversation starter for the next time you guys speak. It's important to remember that when someone is speaking, to listen intently and be genuinely interested in what they are saying. Paying exclusive attention to the person speaking is very important. People love speaking to good listeners. Everyone can sense when someone is engaged and paying attention to what they are saying. If they see you are a good listener they will come back to you when they need someone to talk to.

All these strategies are great ways to make friends, but as long as you're a genuine person that isn't self-centered and actually cares about others, people will like you and want to be your friend. Now the problem I see with many exchange students is that because they are such amazing cool people and have many friends back home, they have never had difficulty making friends in the past. This is a problem because they grew up with the same people and friends and are therefore not used to being put in a situation where they are forced to make new friends. I witnessed this first hand. There is a simple solution to it. YOU HAVE TO TALK TO OTHER PEOPLE. You can't expect others to come up to talk to you, and you respond with one-word responses every time. That's basically telling them to go away. When someone comes up to talk to you, for the love of god, talk to them back. This got me so angry on my exchange because I would see the Italians talk to the other exchange students, and the exchange students would seem like they had never had a conversation with another human being before. I completely understand that you might not either know the language, or that you are just really shy in the beginning and uncomfortable because you're scared and everything is so overwhelming. But you have to absolutely snap out of that mindset because that mindset is what destroys your experience from living the best exchange life you can possibly live.

You have to remember, most of these natives attach themselves to you because they see you as the "cool kid on the block" for the time being. Live up to their expectations and show them that you are indeed someone interesting to be around. When they ask, share cool stories that you've had back home in your home country and they will begin to be more hooked not only to you as a person but the new life you bring to them and their city. They live in a routine life and so anything new in their lives is interesting to them.

Haven't you noticed that the exchange students that have so many friends and are super cool with the natives are almost always the most outgoing ones? All you have to do is talk to other people, and put yourself out there. If you can talk to other people, especially when they come up to you first, they will want to continue to talk to you because in their eyes you are different. This means you provide value and offer something different to them than what they are used to. These people want to have something different in their lives and change up their normal everyday life routine, especially people in a small town.

If you can't talk to other people because of the language barrier all you have to do is learn the language (as many other exchange students have done in the past) or try your best to speak it. As difficult as this is, it's an expectation of you before you go abroad that can be the main factor in determining how many friends you have. In the beginning of the year it is completely ok to suck at the language so you shouldn't feel bad. If you just try and show others that you are actively trying to speak it with them and are trying to learn it they will understand.

The number one mistake why exchange students can't make friends is this. And pay close attention because it happens in almost every district every year. Many exchange students think that they are entitled to everyone else's friendship. They go into their exchange believing that other people are going to come up and talk to them and automatically be friends with them. That is not how it works. This is an absolute improper and toxic mindset. If you have this mindset you are screwed from the beginning. You have to show people you are cool enough and interesting enough that they will want to talk to you again and even hang out with you outside of school. What does end up happening is that all these exchanges students enter their country believing everyone is going to come up and magically be their friend because they are from a different country. So they never go out and talk to other people first and initiate the conversation. This is especially prevalent with students doing their exchange in the United States. A lot of the times too, many people will come up to you and ask about where you're from and how you are enjoying your exchange so far and not many people take advantage of this. You absolutely have to take advantage of this if it happens to you. Many people think once the conversation is over they will come back and talk to them again first because they feel entitled to their friendship, or they just hope they will talk to them again because they are too shy to initiate the next conversation themselves. Keep the conversation going for as long as you comfortably can and be kind and as charismatic as possible. Everyone wants to be friends with the exchange student, but there is no rule that says they have to. So be a cool normal person and keep that friendship alive. This means every time you see that one person, always say hi to them and ask them how they are doing. Remember their name, and say, "Hey (their name)" in the hallways of school or in the city. This creates familiarity with the other person, which will make them more comfortable around you and will lead to more conversations and a closer relationship.

With all that being said, yes, there are some people that will continually come up and talk to you and try to make a strong effort to be your friend. Many people do experience this on their exchange. But if you believe everyone is like this you are wrong. With no matter who you are talking to, you need to have the mindset that it is up to you to put yourself out there and make friends. I know this may sound harsh, but I have seen way too many exchange students be lonely on their exchange because they felt entitled to friendships. This may also make you feel uncomfortable if you are a naturally introverted person, but just because you are reading this right now I know you demand a greater experience from your exchange and are willing to try and make that change. It's just like in life, if you want to change and get better results in all areas of your well-being you have to be willing to put yourself in uncomfortable situations. Thus, if want to have many friends you must be willing to put yourself out there and do things that may make you uncomfortable at times.

CREATING YOUR GROUP OF FRIENDS

Now let's say you've done all these things and have found yourself very popular among your peers. You know many people and have many friends. There is one more thing I want you to keep in mind that's very important.

You need to create a great group of friends to surround yourself with. You become the 5 people you hang around with most, so who you decide to spend most of your time with is very important. Spending a lot of time with certain people will make you subconsciously pick up the habits they have. This can be a good thing or bad thing. Surround yourself with a good group of positive, uplifting people and it's a good thing. Surround yourself with people who are very rude, pessimistic, and maybe even abuse drugs and it's a bad thing. If you develop poor habits on your exchange because of the people you hang out with like smoking, drugs, and excessive drinking you are putting your exchange in danger by risking getting sent home and potentially harming yourself. Even minor habits, like always staying home and playing video games with a friend constantly is bad. It keeps you from going out and experiencing more on your exchange. Be smart with who you decide to spend most of your time with.

You are heavily influenced by your close group of friends. You want to surround yourself with people that are helpful to you on your journey through your exchange. People who are patient with you and help you learn the language. People that are always positive and are living life to the fullest by always wanting to experience great things and want you to have the best time on your exchange. At the end of your exchange, you will look back on the times spent with your friends. If you had a great group of friends you will feel extremely blessed and grateful for them looking back at those experiences. Those experiences you look back on will make you feel a certain way based on who you were with during those times. One of the most important lessons I learned during my exchange was that when I traveled around or went on an adventure, who I went with was more important than where I went. I had more fun on trips to small cities a couple of hours away than on trips to different European countries because of the company I was with.

Summary:

- Put yourself in situations where you are forced to meet new people. Join organizations, clubs, sports teams, etc…

- DO NOT expect others to come up and talk to you. Do not think you are entitled to other people's friendship just because you are an exchange student. You have to take the initiative and go up and talk to other people.

- If the language barrier is a problem, don't worry. You can express more about yourself through your body language than verbal communication. Be optimistic and enthusiastic and connect with others through your body language.

My experience:

My experience with making friends was very easy for a few reasons. Fortunately for me, I was sent to a small city called Cremona. This worked to my advantage because in small cities nothing exciting ever happens. Everyone knows each other, and everyone continues on with their daily routine that they have had for as long as they can remember. So to come into this city as an exchange student, and in my case an American, I was already well liked by many people before I even met them. Many people in my city (and all over Europe in fact) love America and dream of going there someday. So to them, I was a physical representation of their dream, and therefore I was already well-liked by many of them. This did help a lot, but the second and most important reason why making friends came easy to me, was because I applied everything I showed you on how to get people to like you more with everyone I met on my exchange. I read many books before my exchange and learned all these tactics. Therefore, I went into my exchange already knowing them, BUT it wasn't enough to just know these principles, I actually had to apply them as well.

I was always enthusiastic when I met people. I tried my best to radiate positive energy and excitement to others to show them I was so happy to be in Italy. When I spoke to people, I was genuinely interested in what they had to say. I always asked questions about Italy and its rich culture and history, and the Italians loved that I was so curious about it. I also tried to get people to talk to me about themselves, and related to them as much as I could. And when the conversation was over I always made sure to tell them that it was so great to meet them and I hoped to see them around again sometime soon. I would say goodbye at the end of the conversation using their name, to show them that I remembered their name, and when I would talk to people again I had already met I would say, "Hey _____" and call them by their name to show I still hadn't forgotten. They couldn't believe I remembered their name, and it made them feel really special. If they asked how I was able to remember their name I would say something like, "Yea we had a great conversation, I loved talking to you how could I forget your name." And they would find that very nice and flattering.

One thing I did as well, that many other exchange students didn't was that I went out of my way to meet people. I taught myself to have enough confidence to put myself out there, and meet people all around me. I had a goal to try and meet as many people as quickly as I could. I was just so genuinely excited to be on exchange in Italy that I felt like nothing could bring me down. I wasn't afraid of rejection or embarrassment. I was just living life and having a great time. All this helped so much that early on some of the exchange students seemed to get envious of me and would ask me how I already knew so many people within the first couple of weeks. By the second week of my exchange, my Italian friends started calling me "The King of Cremona" because according to them I knew 'everybody'. Obviously, I didn't know everybody, but I had met so many people within the first couple of weeks that I would always see people I knew either in the school hallways or out in the city and say hi them. Later on midway through the year, many of my Italian friends would even make fun of me because they said I knew more people in the city than they did, and they had lived there their whole lives.

All I was doing was being charismatic with the people I met and as a result people wanted to be around me. Every day I would go out of my way during the school break times and go meet people from different classes. Then when I would see those people again the following days, I would go say hi and try to talk to them. When I would go out with my friends at night, every time I saw someone I knew I tried to say hi and even went up to talk to them if I could. If they were in a group of friends that I didn't know I would introduce myself to them too. I became well known not only within my school, but throughout the other school as well and throughout my community. I got interviewed twice on TV for the city, and had a whole page to myself on the city newspaper which explained my life as an exchange student. I'm not saying this to show you how 'cool' I was on my exchange, but I'm saying this merely to show you that it is very possible to have many friends on your exchange and be surrounded by people you love.

All I did was put myself in as many situations as possible to meet people and tried to act charismatic towards the ones I met so they would want to be my friend. What troubled me was that many of the exchange students with me in my city were all so puzzled on how I met so many people, but when I would see them interacting with the Italians I knew exactly why they weren't making friends. In the beginning of the exchange I would be introducing my Italian friends to the other exchange students, and we'd all go out for a drink or a bite to eat. My Italian friends would try to be nice and have conversations with some of the exchange students (in English) and they always responded with one-word answers that would immediately kill the conversation. They rarely asked questions back, and didn't seem interested in the conversation at all. There was no excitement or energy coming from the exchange students. It was clear my Italian friends were persistently trying to start conversations and get to know the exchange students better, but they would always respond as if they hated their life there and just wanted to go back home. Later, my Italian friends would tell me, "Yo, I'm trying to be nice to them, but it just seems like they just don't want to talk to me". I then talked to the exchange students about it and they said they were just shy, because they didn't know them too well. I honestly didn't even know what to do, because I knew the exchange students really well, and they were all super cool. Then, when it came down to meeting people they didn't know, they would turn into completely different people. It's perfectly normal to be shy when you first meet people, but if you are going on exchange you must learn to how to talk to people, especially if they are trying hard to become your friend. If you are naturally shy, practice breaking out of it. This is why you are on exchange, to learn and grow as a person. To develop yourself into who you want to be, and what better place to do that than somewhere with people you will never see again after a year.

Chapter 5: Making school a great experience

The school you attend can play a huge role in determining your happiness on your exchange. Many students struggle with making school a great experience for them, and it's not always their fault. For example, from what I have observed, the U.S. school system may make it tougher to fit in as opposed to other schools like in Europe. Every school has different teachers, different methods of doing things, different students, different classes, different sports coaches, different everything. In the same country or even the same city, you will not find two schools that are identical to each other because of one underlying factor - they all have different people in them.\

The goal is to create a life within your school where you are actually excited to go because you get to see your friends, and you get to experience something different and fun. You do not want to be trapped inside an environment where you are constantly studying, and on top of that have no friends to help you overcome the struggle. Every student, every country, and every situation is different. For example, I didn't need to take classes in Italy because I didn't know one word of the language, and I had already graduated high school back home. But there are many other students going on exchange that actually have to get good grades and try hard in school. That's ok, but don't make school something you dread going to.

BALANCING SCHOOL WORK AND FUN

If you are on your exchange don't let your school work consume your life. I would actually suggest sacrificing a little bit of the grades you make if it meant you would enjoy your experience abroad more. I'm not saying fail a class. I'm saying, if you're deciding on a Saturday night whether you should go hang out with some friends or study for your test Monday, I would rather you chose to give up a few hours of studying to hang out with your friends instead. Do what is fun and do what will make you happy. You are only on exchange one time in your life, and if you're letting Algebra II get in the way of that, you're living it completely wrong. Just give up sleep and try to study late at night or early in the morning if you absolutely have to. Here is a general rule to live by when you are conflicted and deciding on what to do. This is something I live by and remind myself all the time.

In 10 years you will remember the nights you went out and did something fun, not the nights you stayed and slept in.

It's all about finding that healthy balance, but if you must, prioritize your exchange experience first. If you have the option to choose, take the easiest classes and the most interesting ones. They won't make you miserable and they aren't very time consuming, which will free up your time to actually immerse yourself in the culture.

SURROUND YOURSELF WITH THE RIGHT PEOPLE

You always want to try to be around people you already know and like. Let's assume you have found a great group of friends from school because you followed what I told you in the previous chapter. Simple mundane things during school like sitting with your friends, eating lunch with them, and walking to class with them all of a sudden are actually pretty fun. They will immediately make all the difference in your everyday school life. However, don't be limited to only the group of people you know. You should always seek new friends and always talk to new people to grow your circle of influence. The more people you know, the more fun school will be. Just put yourself out there. You have an excuse, you are an exchange student. No one else has that excuse. If an interaction goes completely wrong and is awkward all you have to say is sorry, I am an exchange student I just moved here from [insert country here] and you are immediately forgiven.

Most of the time, who you are surrounded by determines more fun you have, than what you are actually doing. Just sitting in class laughing with a good buddy of yours is much more fun, than skipping class to be by yourself. Surround yourself with people you like, and people who make you feel good. Set a goal to meet someone in each one of your classes. After you've done that, set another goal to meet someone else in those classes. Grow your influence slowly and always be on the lookout to befriend people you spend a large amount of your day with at school. Even getting to know the teachers can be very beneficial. Get close with your teachers, and invest in that relationship with them. They are a valuable asset to have, and your life can only be easier if you have a good relationship with your teacher. Who knows, they might even let a couple of assignments and responsibilities slide because they understand where you are coming from.

FINDING A COMMUNITY WITHIN YOUR SCHOOL

Another great way of actually enjoying school is getting involved or being a part of something that you enjoy. For example, joining the school sports team, or joining theatre, or even the debate club. You want to find a club or community that you like doing, so you can surround yourself with people that enjoy doing the same things. You meet people with similar interests and it's a good way to make new friends. It also makes the school seem a lot smaller and less overwhelming. For example, if you join the basketball or soccer team, you have those group of buddies you can become friends with. You are constantly playing with each other and having fun doing so, which creates a stronger bond between you guys. You might get close to the people on your team, and if you do you might soon find yourself always hanging out with them. Whether you are eating lunch with them, walking to class with them, or hanging out on the weekends with them. You might see your teammates or the members of your club in the hall, and if they say hi to you, you feel good and reassured because you know people. You have found a small community of people you know and have expanded your circle of friends. Now, what seemed to be like a big school suddenly shrinks little by little because you are starting to see more people you know.

If you are doing an exchange in a country that doesn't have school sports or activities like many schools in Europe. Join a club team. It still creates a community for you and makes the city a lot smaller when you go out to the city centre and are able to recognize people you know. Always get involved in anything you can. It will help keep you busy doing something you enjoy doing.

SWITCHING SCHOOLS

Finally, if you absolutely don't enjoy your school whatsoever, for whatever reason, consider talking to your host family, counselor, supervisor, or district to consider changing schools. I know this a lot easier to do in the European and South American countries, but it's definitely possible anywhere if you are absolutely miserable. Let's say you are getting bullied, and you don't have any friends, and the school work and tests are unreasonably difficult for you. Talk to someone who has the power to move you and give them a good reason to consider it.

For example, in Italy each school specializes in teaching a certain topic and students decide on which school to attend depending on what they want to pursue in their career after high school. Therefore, there is a school that specializes in teachings it's students math and science, another one for learning languages, another one for learning how to cook etc.. If you don't like what you are studying, asked to be moved to a different school so you can actually study what you want to do with your future. I know for my district, us exchange students had no say in what school we got put into, so this could be a very good reason to want to change, or a very good excuse if you are absolutely having the worst experience in your current school. Don't abuse the power however. Do it if it's necessary.

Location could also be a good argument. Let's say you switched host families, and now live on the opposite side of town. You used to walk/ride your bike to school, but now it's too far and your parents can't drive you. Your supervisors will definitely listen to what you have to say. If it's too much of a hassle going to and from school, you might be able to get away with a change of location.

If you just really don't like your whole school experience at all in general, talk to your host parents. If you have a good relationship with them, which will always benefit you when you need help, they will likely go out of their way to help you. Communicate with them and let them know you just don't enjoy it there. Maybe you tried everything you could to make friends and meet people and it didn't work, or people and teachers aren't nice to you because you're new or foreign. Talk to your family and let them know what is going on, and that it's greatly affecting your experience. They might be able to talk to your exchange counselor or supervisor to get you to move schools. Let them know how you feel, and more often than not, they will go out of their way to help you.

For many, switching schools is the cop-out way of changing your situation if the only problem you have is that you're uncomfortable there because you don't know people. And there is nothing wrong with that. You have to do what you have to do in order to have a better experience abroad, but I don't want you to fall back on this because being able to switch schools for no reason at all doesn't happen very often in most countries. You can definitely try to change schools, but don't rely on that solution because chances are you won't get switched for something minor like not having many friends. And certainly don't get upset if your program doesn't accept your request. There definitely are situations where the best option is to try and switch, but almost all the time it is because you don't like the life you have set up for yourself in your school. Instead of thinking about switching schools focus your energy on making your current school a better experience. Be grateful for your current situation because many exchange students struggle with serious problems in their schools like bullying and discrimination, and if something like this is happening to you, definitely talk to someone to figure out your situation.

Like I said however, don't expect a switch just because you aren't comfortable there. I have seen it many times before. Exchange students are really quiet in the beginning of the school year because they are shy and nervous and don't know the language so they isolate themselves from everybody else, hoping someone will come talk to them. As a result, they make no friends and become frustrated over time requesting a change in schools. This is not the mentality we talked about in the beginning. No one is going to feel sorry for you. If you don't try and put yourself in uncomfortable situations to create the life you envision yourself having in your year abroad, you will not succeed. You won't be satisfied with the number of friends you have in school, and you are going to find cop-out excuses for things like changing schools hoping it will make things better just because you didn't make an effort to put yourself out there and meet new people. However, if you like your alone time and don't particularly want many friends, then more power to you, keep doing you. As long as you're happy and have no complaints then you're on the right path.

Summary:

- Give up a few hours of studying to hang out with your friends if you have to. In 10 years you will remember the nights you went out and did something fun, not the nights you stayed and slept in.

- Find a good group of friends to surround yourself with during school. Usually who you are with is more important than what you are actually doing.

- Get involved. A big school can be very overwhelming, but joining a team or club can make the school feel a lot smaller as you start to recognize people around the halls or even out in the city.

My experience:

I had the best school experience I honestly could have asked for. I am being 100% honest and not exaggerating. Everything was perfect for me. I went to a language school and got placed in the 4th out of 5 levels and was in the same class with the same 24 people the whole year. In Europe you stay in the same classroom with the same classmates, and only the teachers move from room to room teaching their respective subject. This could either be really good or really bad. But I loved everybody in my class, so it was good for me.

During the first day of school, one of the lady's from the front office took me to my classroom right as class had just started and introduced me to the whole class saying I was an exchange student from Texas and I was going to be their new classmate for the year. After she introduced me, I sat down right in the front in the only open desk available. I quietly sat down and just listened to what the professor in the classroom was saying for two hours. I did not understand any of it because I didn't know Italian right? Well yeah, I went through two hours of lecture thinking this teacher was teaching the class something in Italian, when in fact I found out it was French class and the professor was speaking French the entire time. Yup.. it was at that moment I realized how screwed I was.

Anyways, our school hours were 8:00 a.m. to 1:00 p.m. Monday through Saturday. Every day, every class in the school is given a 15-minute break after the second hour and the fourth. So every class gets a break around 10:00 a.m. and 12:00 p.m.

Therefore, after the two hours of French were over, it was our break time, but I didn't know it. The clock struck 10:00 a.m., and I looked back to see everyone getting out of their chairs so I got up as well. When I got up, I realized they were all getting up to come introduce themselves to me. Every single one of them. They all came up to me one by one in a straight line and introduced themselves in English (because I am at a language school) with the biggest smiles on their face. It totally caught me off guard. They all seemed very excited to have me in their class. To them, I was some super cool exchange student from America and I just so happened to be in their class. They wanted to know everything about me and become my best friend. It was a big deal to them. After I introduced myself to all of them, a few of them grabbed my desk from the front of the room and took it to the back so I could sit with them. After that, they even grabbed my hand and eagerly dragged me around the school to give me a tour and meet other people in other classes during the break. At that moment, while I was walking down the halls with them, I knew I was going to really enjoy my school experience this year.

They helped me with absolutely everything I needed help with. They helped me meet their other friends in the school and they helped me communicate with the teachers that didn't speak English. They helped me convince my teachers I didn't need to be doing work, considering my special circumstances of already completing high school, and so I didn't have to do any work all year long. Never did I turn in one assignment or take one test. I just studied Italian, read my books, and would visit other classes where my other friends were at.

This is why it is super important to be charismatic and have people like you. I got to know the other English teachers in the school really well, and they really seemed to like me. So, they all wanted me to come visit their classes when they were teaching English, and just talk to the class and be there with them while they gave lectures. I even began teaching English and giving presentations because according to them I was the best English speaker in the entire school, and definitely the only one with an American accent. They saw that as very valuable and always wanted me to speak to the students, especially the younger ones who weren't familiar with an American accent.

I got so close to all the teachers in the school, not only the English teachers. In fact, many of them would contact the professor that I was supposed to be with in my original class, and asked them if I could join their specific class to teach English or to just chill. There were days where I would only go to one of my classes, and the other 4 class periods I would spend with my friends in their own classes regardless of the grade level or subject.

I'm telling you, if you make friends not only with the students, but with the teachers as well, by being polite, caring, and most importantly charismatic, opportunities will begin to open to you that you didn't think were there before.

Essentially, I had the ideal school situation and experience. I knew everybody in the whole school because I would meet anyone I could by going from class to class. I was really nice to the teachers, so they never gave me a hard time. They would, in fact, help me with whatever I needed help with. I didn't have to study anything in class which gave me the time to learn Italian and do whatever I wanted. And because I was basically apart of all the classes, I was invited to every class' end of the year field trip. Every class at the end of the year plans a field trip to an exotic place whether in Italy or another country, and they all invited me to go with them. So, because I knew all these people I was able to travel to Greece, France, and parts of Italy with many different classes. I would have gone on more trips with other classes, but many of them overlapped and were expensive. I am pretty sure I missed all but one or two days of school in April because I was just traveling around to different places on these school trips.

You might think I got lucky, and yes I did, but if I was lazy and wanted to, I could have been perfectly content with only knowing the people in my original class. I wouldn't have to get out of my comfort zone, and I could just hang out with the 24 friends I had in my class. But this isn't the mentality you should have if you want to live the best year of your life. Instead, I saw an opportunity to get to know every single person in the whole school and I did. Granted it was not that big of a school, I'm pretty sure almost every person there knew who I was. There were 5-grade levels each containing about 6 classes each with roughly 25 students. That's about 750 people who knew who I was and that I was friends or acquaintances with. I knew almost everybody when I would walk in the halls during our break and talked to anyone I possibly could. I went out of my way to talk to people I had not yet talked to before. I didn't care whether they were in the first year or the fifth year of the high school. I made it a point to talk to everyone, because I was working on growing my circle of friends to as wide as I possibly could. That was my goal. And once I covered the majority of my school I even started visiting my friends in other schools and tried to get to know people in those schools. I told my friends in the other schools to introduce me to their teachers and when they did I proposed I would give a presentation to their class with my American accent, to teach English to them as well. I gave a presentation about my life and my culture back in the U.S. and even if I didn't have an American accent they would have still let me do it, because I was teaching a class about a completely different culture many of them knew absolutely nothing about. As a result, I got to know students in other schools and grew my circle even larger.

Do you see what I'm getting at? I had a vision of how I wanted my exchange to go, and that vision involved being well known within my city and community because I knew it would lead to more open doors and opportunities for a better exchange. I didn't wait for people to come up and talk to me, I went out and did what I could to meet people. I created opportunities for myself, many others would have never seen in the first place.

I had the mentality that each person I met wanted to get to know me. I believed I was special and had something to offer because I was from a different country and I believed everyone wanted to be my friend even if they didn't. I knew my value as a person and I knew I could be a good friend to anyone I met, and because I truly believed that, I had zero problem going up to someone I had never met before and getting to know them. And when I did do that, more often than not, they already knew who I was because people talked about the new exchange students in the city. And if they didn't know who I was they would recognize my accent and be super interested in what I had to say because I was an American boy learning how to speak Italian.

People talk a lot, so if you are kind and just a genuine person to someone, people will go tell their friends and family about the "super cool exchange student guy/girl" they met that day. I learned that very quickly in Italy. People talk about you, even if you think they aren't talking about you. And that could be a good thing or a very bad thing, so be smart and be kind to every person you meet. Doesn't matter their age, gender, ethnicity, or religion just be kind and people will always want to be around you.

Again I know all this may sound very conceited. I am not saying this to boast, sound cocky, or show what I accomplished because it makes me feel good about myself. I don't care about that stuff anymore. My exchange is over, and I'm never going back to it. But you still have yours to live. I enjoyed my time, and all I want now is to help you enjoy yours.

Chapter 6: Take advantage of every opportunity

One thing you might have noticed from my experiences abroad was that I always took advantage of every opportunity. I believe I did this well, and because of it I created many more unforgettable memories, built longer-lasting relationships with people I met, and lived the best possible year I could have imagined. It is very important to take advantage of every opportunity that comes knocking on your door. Sometimes you may not even recognize the opportunity, but you must learn to see them when they present themselves. Other times you may recognize the opportunity, but may not feel like taking advantage of it because you feel tired or lazy. If you truly want to create most of what you are given to work with, you must take advantage of every opportunity.

An opportunity is a situation or a circumstance that can yield big rewards in terms of making your time abroad much more unforgettable and enjoyable. Results of taking advantage of opportunities include happiness, peace of mind, friendship, love, fun times, unforgettable memories, and much more.

So here are some things you can do to take advantage of opportunities on your exchange:

1. ALWAYS SAY YES

When someone asks you to do something you should always say yes! Even if the task is boring and takes away from your own personal time. Many of the times the task is in fact is the way that it seems - boring and stupid as you would have thought, but many times something good comes out of it.

For example, let's say you're watching Netflix and your host mom asks you to go to the grocery store. First off, anytime your host parents ask you to do something, you should do it, and with a good attitude as well. You need them to like you. It is very important. But let's say you're really into your show and the good part is coming on, and you're so invested in the show that you really don't want to be doing anything else. However, your host mom asks you to go to the grocery store, what do you say? Yes. You say yes. You can always finish the show later and there are so many possible rewards that could come out of doing something so meaningless. For example, your host mom will appreciate you more and you guys will gain a stronger bond as a result. Who knows you might even meet some new people and make friends on the walk to the store (for all the people living in Europe) or at the store. You can even learn all about the produce your host country produces and even use that time to learn so much about the culture. Any mundane or meaningless activity you do back home, is a whole new experience in your host country so don't be afraid to go do it.

Another example is, you are feeling tired and all you've wanted to do all day is sleep, but your friends ask you to go out to the city center or downtown with them that night. You have to say yes. Suck it up, you can sleep tomorrow or on the weekend. You don't know how many people I have met by hanging out with my friends, specifically when I didn't initially want to go out. So many great things have happened to me from situations that I have said yes to. I have made close friends that way, that have later, invited me to go on crazy exotic trips with them and their family (look in "My Experience" to read an example). The possibilities are endless for you if you always say yes. You do more, you experience more, and you fully immerse yourself in the culture. Many good things come to those who are always optimistic and down to do things when others ask them to.

Side note: Obviously, it goes without saying, make sure the things you are saying yes to are not illegal or dangerous.

2. DON'T FORGET TO HAVE FUN

The reason why you are on exchange is to learn about a different culture, learn a new language, and grow as a person all simultaneously while having fun. If you are not having fun, then what are you even doing. You can learn about the world and about yourself all while having fun. Enjoying your time abroad is the most important thing to do. That's what this whole book is about - to get you to try and enjoy your time abroad as much as you possibly can.

You might be thinking, "Of course Andy. All I want to do is have fun, why else would I be here if I didn't want to have fun." Well let me tell you, it's not about wanting to have fun, it's about forgetting to have fun. While you are abroad whether you are studying, or are there for a cultural exchange. Responsibilities and concerns might start hitting you. School becomes a huge distraction, and it makes students forget that they are adventuring in another country for crying out loud.

Other times, during an exchange, you might get in a fight with one of your friends or another exchange student or even start falling for someone that doesn't like you back. Regardless of what it is, you get hurt by someone, and you become depressed, and begin to stay home or keep to yourself. Before you know it, valuable time passes by and you were to busy worrying about the past that you forgot to make the most of what was right in front of you, and you miss an opportunity.

I have seen many of my friends abroad miss out on making many new friends and going out with exchange students, because they were dwelling on someone specifically during their exchange that had them distracted. On your exchange you will go through a roller coaster of emotions, and only you have the power to discipline yourself enough to understand that your time there is limited. If you don't become deeply aware with the fact that you will leave soon, and will never be able to return, you will learn not to dwell on things that will keep you from having fun and experiencing all your exchange has to offer.

3. TRAVEL WHENEVER YOU CAN

I know almost all exchange programs have restrictions when it comes to traveling around your host country. I am not telling you to go against the rules, I am just telling you that whenever you have the opportunity to go somewhere new, or anywhere out of your hometown at all, you should definitely do it. You are in a new country with more than just your host city to experience, and you need to look for new ways to get out and see more of that country whenever you can. Ask your parents, ask your friends, ask your exchange program. You are, by default, traveling already just by being on your exchange, but the world is vast and I promise you wherever you go, there are places around you that would be a great opportunity to experience. Traveling brings joy and happiness to the adventurous spirit in you, so you must not settle by staying in your city the entire year.

I always tried finding new ways to travel around Italy, and even Europe for that matter. My district was very strict when it came to traveling alone, so the only way students in our district were allowed to travel were either with Rotary, host families, or other adults with Rotary's consent. Not to mention Rotary only planned two trips the whole year for us, and my parents worked every weekday which limited me greatly. However, that should be no reason to stop trying. Even with the strict rules I was able to travel to almost every major city in all of Italy and even Greece, France, Germany, Switzerland, and the Netherlands during my exchange.

I was able to travel around Italy just by putting myself out there and asking around for different opportunities to travel. I asked my host parents, my friends, Rotary counselors, Rotex students (past Rotary exchange students), and even my classes from my school that went on field trips during the year. I visited France and Germany with two separate classes from my school, by simply asking the professors of those classes. I told them that I would never be in this situation again to travel around such a beautiful continent with an organized class that had students I was already familiar with. It was a once in a lifetime opportunity and I would greatly appreciate their consideration to bring me on board… They agreed.

Then I visited around Italy, with my host family, Italian friends (after asking Rotary), Rotary themselves, and other class trips that I asked permission for as well. I visited Rome my second month in Italy, because my host dad had a business trip there and I asked to come with him, and he was happy to bring me along. I visited the other countries in Europe as well by doing a week-long road trip with one of my host families after simply asking them to come along with them. They were already planning the trip to visit a University in The Netherlands for my host brother, and they thought it was a good idea for me to tag along. We made a few extra stops in other countries as well so they could show me around to new places.

The point is, I took advantage of any opportunity I could to travel. I put myself out there, and it actually worked, even with the strict rules my district placed on us exchange students. Granted, I did get shot down by Rotary many times when I asked to travel, but I kept asking and some of the times they said yes. As a result, I left Italy visiting every city I had on my list before I arrived.

Some of the times you will get rejected when asking to travel, and that's ok, I got rejected many times. But the main point is to always be on the lookout for those opportunities and to never stop asking. If you do that I promise, you will visit places you wouldn't have otherwise visited before.

ANOTHER RULE TO KEEP IN MIND

As you can see from the previous points, and the previous chapters for that matter, there is a common theme this book shares if you have not been able to tell:

THE THINGS YOU REGRET THE MOST ARE THE THINGS YOU DIDN'T DO RATHER THAN THE THINGS YOU DID DO.

I'm not saying go out and break the law or do exactly what your exchange program is telling you not to do. Be smart with your decisions. However, when you are contemplating whether or not you should do something, like hanging out with your friends, or going to church with your host parents, in the end, the decisions you regret the most are the things you didn't do, rather than the things you did. Go out and be proactive. That is the most important thing you can do to make the most of your exchange. If you are having a tough time deciding whether or not to do something, just think back to this chapter and go do it. You might be bored in the moment doing the activity, but in the end more times than not, you will look back on it and be glad you have another memory to hold on to. On your exchange it isn't those few big things you did abroad that make up your whole exchange, it's the many little things you did that define it all when you look back on it.

Summary:

- Responsibilities and distractions can hit hard, causing a roller coaster of emotions. But don't let valuable time pass you by because you were too busy worrying about the past that you forget to make the most of the present.

- Always seek new opportunities to travel more. Put yourself out there and ask everyone around. Don't be limited to your own little city.

- No matter how tired or lazy you are feeling, if someone asks you to do something always say yes. The things you regret more are the things you didn't do rather than the things you did do.

My experience:

My whole exchange consisted of taking advantage of many opportunities. I explained a couple above briefly, like traveling to Rome with my host dad, and visiting France and Greece with classes from my school. If you want to see my videos for each of those trips they are on my YouTube channel. Just type in "Andy Serna – Exchange in Italy" and it should take you there.

However I am only going to go over one opportunity here, and it led to an amazing trip later on in my exchange.

One day our rotary district was having a meeting to present the Rotary Youth Exchange Program for all students who potentially wanted to do the exchange the following year as an outbound student. They asked each current exchange student from the city, Cremona, to come to the meeting and introduce ourselves to answer any questions the potential outbounds might have. I really did not want to go. It meant I would have to sit and wait through a presentation I had already heard many times before, and this time in another language. However, as much as I didn't want to go, I forced myself too, because I really did try to have the mindset of doing new things that weren't a part of my daily routine as boring as they sounded.

I decided to go, and we all introduced ourselves at the beginning of the Rotary presentation by saying our name and where we're from. I sat through the presentation while the Youth Exchange Officer explained everything about the exchange program. I was bored out of my mind. After a couple of hours, the meeting finally ended and while I was walking out the door to walk back home, a lady that was in the audience by herself, quickly grabbed my arm and stopped me before I could get away. Her name was Monica Tonoli. One of my favorite people to this day. She introduced herself and asked me where exactly from Texas I was from. I told her I was from San Antonio, and that I would be attending Texas A&M University the following year for my college career. She then went on to tell me her son, Carlo, who was about a year younger than me visited Texas a few times before and stayed in the dorms of the A&M campus twice, as part of a short exchange he did himself. I could not believe it. Not many people from Italy, get out and leave the country as such a young age, especially to the U.S, let alone Texas. Texas is almost like a country of its own. It has its own culture and is extremely big. And to find out someone from Italy, had stayed at the University I was about to attend the following year blew my mind. So we kept talking, and she then asked if she could give Carlo my contact information. Of course I said yes and a few days later he texted me.

He invited me to hang out with him and his friends from school, and even invited me to watch a few basketball games with him of the city team. He was very Americanized and I could tell he loved hanging out with me because I was a physical reminder of the great times he had in America when he was there. We got along very well. He quickly became one of my good friends in Cremona.

One night he invited me to have a nice dinner with him and his family at his house, so I could meet them all and see his mom again. I went and we had an amazing dinner all together. One of the nicest families I have ever met. We all got along very well. We had great conversations and we learned a lot about each other.

While I was there eating my pasta they proposed an idea to me. They began by telling me they own a cabin a few hours north in the northern mountains of Italy. They go and stay there almost every winter to go skiing. Then, they proceeded to ask me if I wanted to go with them that winter. I was ecstatic that they would even consider on their own to let me come with them. Like I said earlier, it was very hard to travel considering my district had strict rules. But Carlo's parents knew Giorgio, my Youth Exchange Officer, personally and the fact that I would be going with a family he was familiar with meant I would probably be able to go on the trip with them. They called him the next week and he approved.

Therefore, for a week that winter, they took me to their cabin in the gorgeous Alps of Northern Italy. We ventured through the mountains together, skied together, and they paid for all my meals and everything I needed to enjoy myself while I was there. I could not have been any more grateful that they thought of me, and allowed me to have that experience of a lifetime. I had skied before in Colorado, but the Italian mountains were something different. I just remember skiing down a slope surrounded by the most beautiful mountains I had ever seen scaling all around me all the way up to the sky. And all this happened because I went to a Rotary meeting I almost didn't go to because I *didn't feel like it.*

To this day I still keep in contact with Carlo and his family. He was one of my best friends in Italy and still is. In fact, after my first year in College, my brother and I traveled all through Europe that summer and Carlo and his dad just so happen to be in Prague for that month that we were traveling. They had their own place in downtown Prague, and while we were traveling he asked us to come visit him while he was there. How could we decline the offer? As a result, during our Europe extravaganza we took a detour and visited Carlo and his dad in Prague for about 5 days and did not pay a penny to stay with them in their temporary home smack dab in the center of downtown Prague. I got to visit Prague without having to pay for a place to stay downtown, and Carlo and I had the opportunity to catch up as old pals once again.

That my friend is the potential of just doing something, you don't feel like doing.

.

Chapter 7: Bring your culture with you

When you are in your host country you'll see that people will come up to you and say hi because they find out you're from a different country. This is true not only because they want to get to know the new guy/girl in town, but because they may rarely be exposed to people from your country and are therefore curious about it and its culture.

You are not the only person learning during your exchange. The people around you, such as friends and families, are trying to learn from you as well.

They are curious and want to know more about your country, the culture in it, the politics, religion, social behaviors and more. And for the first time with many of the people you come in contact with, they finally have a primary resource that could give them those answers - you. Therefore, I highly recommend knowing a bit about your country, specifically the history and politics behind it because YOU WILL have people ask you about those uncomfortable topics when you are abroad. This is especially true if you are from America going to any other country. I learned this from personal experience. People from all around the world are very curious about American life and they will not hesitate to ask you about what you think of the current president, about past historical events, and even controversial topics like for me, the death penalty, since I am from Texas.

This is completely ok. American culture tends to shy away from these topics, but many other cultures embrace these conversations. They are not interrogating you, they simply just want to learn about the culture and customs of where you're from. Depending on where you are from and where you are going this is one particular situation where you might need to adapt and know beforehand before if it catches you off guard. Based off my personal experience I find that in America when people are arguing, many people take it personally. They become very defensive and act as if the person is attacking them personally. When I went to Italy I found people arguing a lot, but no one ever took their arguments personally. They knew that the person they were arguing with was just attacking their argument and not them. So when I found myself in arguments with my Italian friends, I naturally thought they were attacking me personally, but they weren't. I had to adjust and remind myself that it was just the European culture. They engage in many intelligent conversations and arguments and that is why many of them are very clever and intelligent people. I learned all this the hard way, and this is something you should keep in mind before going abroad. Don't take things personally, it's just the cultural barrier.

The best way for these people to get a little bit out of your culture is by asking you questions. And this is good. But I challenge you to bring your culture with you through different experiences. What do I mean by this? If all these people want to do is get to know more about your cultural background and the country you're from, I challenge you to bring a little bit of your native country to your host country.

Bring back your culture with you to your new friends and host family. You could do this, by making a popular recipe from back home for your family or even teaching them a bit of your language as well. You could pull out a map and show them the geography of everything near your hometown and where you have traveled to in your native country. You could even celebrate a holiday or birthday the way you normally would back home. Find something you do different back home, and use it as a new experience for your friends and family so they could see first-hand the cultural difference between your culture and theirs.

What does this accomplish?

1. Your host friends and family experience and learn something new

Like I've said before, people are tired of the same routine and love experiencing new things, especially if it's from you, someone who they are investing so much time and energy into. They are not just reading about the different traditions from different countries, for once they are actually living it without having to leave their home. That is the value you bring to these people's lives. Once you realize that and utilize it, people will appreciate you more and want to be around you all the time, since you are constantly offering something no one else can't. You bring value into other people's lives, and that is the main recipe to making new friends and living an abundant life on your exchange.

2. It shows you have something to offer them as well.

Your relationship with everyone you meet in your host country is not one-sided. Offer them something no one else can and the relationship becomes mutual which builds stronger connections with people and allows everyone to grow from each other. The relationships you make should not be just you receiving all the time and them giving. Both parties should be learning and growing from each other. Offer them something as well, something their normal friends can't offer. That makes you special and sets you apart on your exchange for every single person you come in contact with.

3. It shows you care

It shows you care enough to let them in your personal life back home and are willing to share your personal experiences and traditions with others who are curious about it. I know for a fact most host families will GREATLY appreciate you sharing your life back home with them through different acts, experiences, and stories. You let them in your life and care enough to go out of your way to make the experience for others around you a great one for them too. This is why they took you in the first place. They are also experiencing something new, by bringing you into their home for a few months. Make sure you don't leave them empty-handed.

Summary:

- You are not the only one trying to learn on your exchange. The people around you want to learn from you as well.

- Know a bit about your country beforehand. Such as the history, politics, and current events, because you will have people ask you about it when you're abroad.

- Find something you do differently back home, like a certain tradition, and use it as a new experience for your host friends and family so they can see the cultural differences between your own culture and theirs.

My experience:

One of the main things that deepened my relationship with my host family, was me introducing them to traditional American experiences. My host mother and I specifically got really close when we cooked food together I would normally eat back home. I think one of the best things you can do to strengthen your relationship with your host parents is to cook together things you would normally make back home. My host mom, like many other moms all over the world, loved to cook, so to be able to introduce new ideas to her was not only a learning experience for her but a fun one for both of us as well. I had many other friends who did this and it worked for them as well.

Unfortunately, I didn't take advantage of this activity because not only did I not know how to cook well, but more importantly I didn't know how powerful it could be when it came to creating a great experience for you and your host family together. That was until my best friend from Mexico, Leo, came to visit me in Cremona and stayed with my host family and I. Leo was also an exchange student in my district with me. He lived in another city however, which was 4 hours away by train. Leo was from Mexico, and Mexico has a very rich culture when it comes to food, just like Italy. Leo also loved to cook, and would cook with his mom back home in Mexico all the time.

Therefore, when Leo came and visited my host family and me in Cremona, he surprised us all by having the idea to make food for us all while he was staying with us. When he had the idea and presented it to my host mom, I would never forget her face. She lit up like a light bulb, and had the biggest smile I ever saw on her. I immediately thought, "Dammit, why hadn't I ever thought of that". Leo then told us, he cooks for his host family back in his city, and they love it every time he makes Mexican food for them. The whole time Leo was making Mexican food for my host mom, she was very excited. She was smiling, laughing, and clapping repeatedly out of joy throughout the whole process. I just remember sitting there at the table analyzing Leo and my host mom getting along in the kitchen as he showed her how to make a popular Mexican dish from his native country. At that time, she seemed to like Leo more than she did me. That was because, for my host mom, her whole life revolved around her cooking. That was the number one thing she took pride in, and rightfully so, I genuinely still think she is the best cook I ever met (right behind my real mom of course). So, from her perspective it made complete sense. An Italian woman, who loved to cook more than anything, and loved to learn about other cultures anytime she could, would obviously appreciate nothing more than someone teaching her a new recipe from a different country on the opposite side of the globe. It was unbelievable what I was witnessing. My host mom instantly clicked with Leo and it was all because he took the time to introduce her to a new dish from his native country. It was the perfect bonding experience for her. She even made a joke at the dinner table, while we were all eating together and told me in Italian, "Andy why can't you be more like Leo." Hahaha say what you will about that statement, but she was right. Even when I was sitting down watching them cook together I even told myself, "Andy why can't you be more like Leo."

Keep this in mind when you are in your host country. The activity does not have to be cooking and it does not have to be with your host family. It could be teaching your friends hot to play a sport, or an instrument, or a board game. It could be anything you do back home, that your host friends or family have not experienced before. Find what those people love and if you can match certain activities you did back home to their particular interests you have struck gold.

Chapter 8: Learn some new hobbies

When you are on exchange you will have a lot of time to yourself. I know I did, especially since I did no school work whatsoever all year long. You are on exchange not just to mess around and have fun, but to learn and grow into someone new. You will begin to mature at an exponential rate and you will develop skills, a certain mentality, and beliefs you would not have if you did not go on exchange. Through all this time and opportunity it is important to take advantage of the new world around you with all the ideas and activities you wouldn't normally be exposed to back home. Don't forget that you are on exchange to become a better person, and develop yourself into someone you want to be.

Therefore what this chapter is about and what I strongly believe every exchange student must do is to learn some new skills and new hobbies you have always wanted to learn, but never got the chance to. Now would be the perfect time. You are in the experimental stage of your life. If there is any time in your life to try and fail at something new, it is now. There is no better time to try new things. This can be anything you want. Learning how to play an instrument, or how to play a certain sport, a new language from another exchange student, or how to cook. Even if you just want to try and read more books, or adopt a specific style of fashion to bring back home with you. Now is the time. Experiment with what you have and learn something that would make you a better and more diverse all around person.

A lot of this is influenced by where you decide to go to on your exchange. For example, if you go to the States that would be a great time to learn a sport, since playing sports are very common for students there. If you decide to go to Italy, that would be a great opportunity to learn how to cook, since Italians put so much cultural and historical emphasis on their cuisine. Even if you are just going anywhere in Europe, it would be a perfect opportunity to learn how to play an instrument, since European cultures revolve heavily around musical talent. If you decide to go to a Scandinavian country, that would be a great time to learn how to sail, ice fish, or partake in any of those common activities in that geographic area. Depending on where you go, you can learn certain things. But many hobbies are just up to you, and how you decide to spend your time.

The hardest part about learning a new hobby is being disciplined enough to schedule out a few minutes of your day to learn it. In the process of learning a new skill, Robert Green talks about in his book "Mastery" that at times it can be very tempting to quit. On your journey to learning something new, you will see certain progress in the beginning and then have a period where you plateau before you see any more progress. It will feel like you have been stuck in the same place for a long time. You will experience this process through learning your new language as well. If you keep pushing through that plateau eventually you will move past that hump and get to the next level. So keep pushing forward and don't give up on what you decide to learn. It will pay off in the long run I promise you that.

Not only is this a good idea as it helps with your personal development, but learning a new hobby also has many other effects. Here are other ways learning a hobby can help you on your exchange.

1. Builds confidence

Learning a hobby builds confidence in an individual. Being able to learn something new and challenging can be very rewarding and gives you a feeling of accomplishment. This will translate to all areas of your life, and you will begin to see a change in how you approach other challenges and obstacles in your exchange.

2. Reduces Stress

It also helps in reducing stress you might have during your exchange. Getting caught up in something you love doing is a great distraction for any problems you might be facing on your exchange. It refocuses your thoughts and energy on something that is helping you grow as opposed to something that is negatively affecting you and keeping you from growing.

3. Leads to more friendships

It also helps with the social aspect of your life. If you learn something new, like an instrument in Europe or a sport in America for example, there will be many people around you that share that similar skill and interest. If you learn how to play an instrument, you can now jam with a group of other people and make friends and build those relationships as well. You can now be a part of a team or group where you are doing something you enjoy, which will definitely lead to a closer relationship with the others in your group. Not only do you have to actively participate in the hobby together, but you will be able to talk about it with anybody else interested in it or anybody that shares the same hobby. It leads to a more meaningful conversation and will definitely lead to a better relationship with that person. I know when I found out I shared a similar hobby with someone I had just met, I tackled that topic and we talked about it for a while and I ended up becoming friends with a lot of people who shared similar interests and did the same things as me. People like people who are similar to themselves so if you start learning things that help you relate to other people, you will without a doubt build not only a lot more friendships, but a lot more meaningful ones as well.

4. Gives you a sense of fulfillment

More importantly however, learning a new hobby gives you a sense of fulfillment. Once you make progress in learning something new, you can literally feel yourself growing and becoming someone new. It provides a tangible way to show you that you are changing into someone new and someone you are actively trying to become. You feel a sense of fulfillment, and through fulfillment, you become happier. You will radiate positive energy wherever you go and this momentum will be a snowball effect to the other areas of your exchange, and there is no better feeling in the world. This is what exchange is all about.

Summary:

- You are in the experimental stage of your life. There is no better time to try and fail at something you have always wanted to do.

- It keeps you busy. You will have a lot of free time on your hands, and there is no better way to spend that time than learning something new.

- It helps with personal development. Learning new things gives you a sense of fulfillment and allows you to grow day after day

My experience:

As I mentioned earlier, school didn't take up much of my time. In fact, it didn't take out any of my time outside of school. So I had a lot of time on my hands especially since everyone else had to study for exams and classes. I took advantage of this and decided not to waste my time. One thing early on in my exchange that had really frustrated me, was I saw that almost every single member of my Italian host family (even the aunts/uncles and cousins) all knew how to play an instrument. Playing an instrument in Italy was like playing sports in America... and I had never even touched one before in my life. I knew I wanted to learn because it's such a great skill to have, I just never really had the time. Well, now I did. I picked up my host dads guitar from home and began first by asking him and my host sister to teach me how to play. At first, they were like "ok yea I would love to teach you", kind of saying it as if they didn't take me seriously. Once I kept asking and literally got the guitar and went up to them to show me a few chords they were shocked and ecstatic to see how serious I was about learning. Instruments is a huge part of the culture in Europe, so showing them I was genuinely interested in fully immersing myself in the culture really gained their respect. They showed me a few chords to get started and I practiced for around 30 minutes a day, sometimes hours. I ended up getting on YouTube and learning from there when my dad and sister weren't home. This helped a lot. YouTube can really teach you anything you want to know.

After being consistent day after day, over time I eventually learned how to play the guitar. My host family even bought me my very own guitar for my birthday which was one of the most thoughtful gifts I had ever received from anybody. I still play to this day and have occasional jam sessions with my roommates in college since they play the guitar as well. Learning an instrument is definitely a lifelong skill worth learning.

Other than learning how to play the guitar I also picked up on another hobby that has impacted my life far greater than I can ever imagine. It's something I love to do and has become part of my identity. I began recording my travels to different cities and different countries with my GoPro and making cool videos/montages of my trip. Some people refer to me as that guy that makes 'cool videos'. They're not great by any means, it just started becoming a part of who I am. It turned out to be a far greater success to me because traveling is something I love to do and will never stop doing. So when I make these videos and go back and re-watch all the memories I've made, I get a certain feeling in my stomach I just can't get from pictures. Videos capture the raw emotion and liveliness of your experience. I created a YouTube channel and put each video on there to easily access and share the videos. I was able to share them with my friends and family in my host country and even with people back home which showed everyone I was truly living my greatest life abroad. I had made a couple of random videos before on small family trips back home just for the heck of it but during my exchange I made about 7 different videos of trips with Rotary, my school, and even just my friends during random weekend trips. It was probably the best thing I did on my exchange no doubt. Even right now, 3 years later, I still go back to my YouTube channel and re-watch all those great videos and memories I shared that I will never forget. I shared them with my Rotary club, Italian friends, and family back home. Everyone was finally able to get a glimpse to the part of my life I simply could not put into words. It even reached out to exchange students and other travelers around the world that somehow were able to find the video. The videos became more popular than I expected. I just posted them for myself, but some of them got around to many other viewers. My Sicily video has over 9000 views and a few other of my videos have over 2000.

Making the videos was easy. I just took a GoPro with me wherever I went and edited each video on a free editing software GoPro provides to everyone called GoPro studio. You can even make videos on iMovie which comes with every Mac computer. You just upload your raw footage, edit the parts you want in your video, and add cool background music. I definitely encourage each and every one of you to do something like this where you can go back and relive your memories whether through videos or photos. You will definitely go back and re-watch them in the future more often than you think.

I also encourage you to visit my channel and see exactly what I am talking about when I talk about the videos I make. I create each one to give the viewer a certain feeling that makes them feel good inside. Go watch my videos and get ideas so you can hopefully be inspired to take your exchange head on or maybe even start your own YouTube channel for yourself one day. I didn't do YouTube to gain subscribers or a lot of views. I did it because it's easy access for me, my friends, and my family to view. Every time I get nostalgic I just go back and re-live those memories through the videos I made.

To find my channel you can just search my name on Youtube: "Andy Serna – Exchange in Italy". And if you'd like, feel free to subscribe as well.

Chapter 9: Falling in love

This chapter is how to deal with falling in love while in your exchange. Before I begin I just want to state that this is a very sensitive topic. Many people in love are in denial about a lot of feelings and criticism they get from the people around them. Therefore, let me remind you, I am not telling you what to do, I am just pointing out what I have experienced in the past with friends of mine falling in love. Obviously, I can't judge your relationship without knowing anything about it. So take my advice with a grain of salt as it may not be applicable to your specific scenario, but may be applicable to many others.

For some, it's inevitable and thus needs to be talked about. The reason why falling in love on your exchange happens so often is because, for the first time for many people, you and many others are on the same journey of your own lives of adventure and experience in figuring out who you truly are as a person. When people are on a journey and their paths cross with someone else on a similar journey, bonds begin to form stronger than anything else and quicker than you could ever imagine. This is the exact reason why your relationships with the people you meet abroad feel so much stronger than any friends you have back home, even though you barely met these people, and knew your friends back home for many years. Love, through attraction or just friendly love, while on your exchange and with your fellow exchange students, is not about time, it's about intensity. And the intensity you feel with someone else amplifies when you are on this journey, in a beautiful country with its gorgeous scenery, surrounded by amazing people while simultaneously feeling completely alone and vulnerable. You two are on the same boat and are at the same point in your life, where you feel free and connected with everything around you. For once, everything in your life seems to be happening for a reason and things start to fall in place.

It can be that everything in your life is perfect, and you are at an all-time high in your life, or you feel lonely and depressed and meet someone else feeling the same way. Regardless, emotions are strong with you and other exchange students, so when you meet someone you would normally barely talk to back home, there's a good chance you will really get along with them on your exchange. This is true with just another native in your host country as well, and not just with other exchange students. For once in your life, your responsibilities and worries are at a minimum, so when you find someone attractive you really like, all your focus and energy is on them. It's hard to distract yourself from that person, considering you're not so busy with academic and career stuff as much as you would be back home.

It's also completely different than meeting someone back home because on your exchange you're not just hanging out with someone in school, or at a house, or a party. Abroad, you are constantly experiencing new things every day and are surrounded by the beautiful culture and scenery you are not used to. This affects your mood and feelings on a day to day basis. You become more self-aware as an exchange student and begin to appreciate even the littlest things in life. So when someone comes along with the same mindset as you, you feel as though you guys belong together. Like it was meant to be. You are on the same wavelength, and your energy matches up perfectly with this other person. There is no way to describe it other than

111

the fact that IT JUST FEELS RIGHT. That's the best way to put it. No one knows why they feel this way with this other person, other than the fact that it just feels right.

Well on your exchange this can be a good thing or a very bad thing. There is a reason why this is one of the 4 D's. That's because falling in love with someone can truly ruin your experience as an exchange student. In the moment everything is perfect and you don't want to have to deal with anything or anyone else in your life other than that person. However, I'm not going to sit here and tell you not to fall in love, because that's irrational as we can't control who we fall in love with. What I am here to tell you is how to deal with it on your exchange.

If you find yourself falling in love with another person, the best thing you can do is take a step back and reflect on the situation. You have to be aware that in that exact moment all you are going to want to do is think about them day and night and forget everything else going on that doesn't have to do with that person. The feeling is almost always temporary, but your experience as an exchange student is forever.

It's ok if you choose to drop everything and be with that one person your entire exchange. My job is to just point out the consequences if you choose to go down that route. I have had many exchange student friends, some from Texas with me that did an exchange in a different country, and other exchange students in my district in Italy, that chose to go down this route and they all greatly later regretted it at the end of their exchange. This happened to one exchange student with me in my city, and once she got a boyfriend we never saw her again, even though the city was extremely small. Our friendship faded, and she never created any memories with us from that point on anymore. She did, however, create many memories with her boyfriend but that's your call to make on which memories you would prefer to have. There have also been cases where I've seen people fall in love on their exchange and continue to date long after their exchange has ended. I have found this to rarely be the case however, but that is completely up to your own judgment on how long you believe your relationship will last.

If you decide to continue dating this person through your exchange, just know that you will miss out on many opportunities to make this year the best year of your life. But who am I to tell you not to be with the person you love right? I don't know exactly how you are feeling towards that person. My only question to you is, are you truly feeling love towards the other person or is it just lust? If you are in love on your exchange and I ask you "Is this person 'The One'"? Because obviously if they are 'The One', then you don't just want to drop them completely. Eight or Nine times out of ten, the exchange students will say yes they are 'The One'. So, it's up to you to decide how you really feel towards this person. Are the feelings temporary or are they the real deal?

There is no right answer on the route you chose to go down, I just want you to make sure if what happens once the year goes by, you find out it didn't work out, and you wonder how you could have been so stupid to waste your entire year abroad with someone alone, rather than being out and experiencing the world for yourself.

But I am not here to tell you to choose either or. I am not saying you either have to drop the person if you want to live the best year of your life or stay with them and face the consequences. I am not about choosing one side or the other. I am all about trying to help you experience everything as best as you can. The key to a successful exchange year and life, in general, is to live in moderation. It's difficult to balance everything as best you can, and not be too consumed in one particular activity or situation.

So here is how to make the most of your exchange while still being in love:

You do not want to let this person come in front of you and the opportunities you have to make this the best exchange year of your life. For example, if you just made a group of friends at school and they ask you to hang out on a Friday night you DO NOT SAY NO because you planned on staying with the person you like. You most definitely go and try to make new friends and new experiences still as much as you can. If you have downtime the next day for example on a weekend or any day of the week you don't have anything going on, then it is ok to hang out with that person at that time. Don't overdo this because you will begin to forget about everything else around you, like your host family, school, and friends.

You do not want to spend all day with this person, or even talking to this person for that matter. Set out a couple of hours a day to meet with this person or even just 4 or 5 days of the week. If they are also an exchange student it helps because you can hang out as a group together and don't have to be isolated just you two. You can even introduce that person to your friend group and include them in you and your friends' daily hangout or vice versa.

It's going to be one of the most difficult things you do to try and limit yourself with this person. If you do in fact feel such strong feelings for the person, then you are not going to want to do anything else except be with that person. And while that might affect your relationships with the other people on your exchange, for some of you, that might be completely worth it. Therefore, at the very least, try to make a deal with this person by coming up with a way to experience the most of the city, the culture, and learning the language together, rather than doing nothing all day and staying in your room. Go out and experience things together. Still, take advantage of the fact that you are in a beautiful country and there is no reason not to try and experience everything it has to offer. Whether you did it alone, with great friends, or someone you love, go out and get a taste of it all, especially now that you're with people you actually enjoy spending time with.

Summary:

- Don't confuse love for lust. If it's not going to be long-term, understand that you are sacrificing your only year abroad for one person that might not mean anything to you in the future.

- If you do decide to stay with the person you love, do it in moderation. Don't let them consume your entire exchange. Balance them and all your other exchange experiences accordingly.

- You're not going to want to do anything else except be with this person. Don't let your love for this person come in front of you and the opportunities you have to make this the best exchange life you can possibly live.

My experience:

A little back story on me. Before leaving for my exchange I had never really liked anybody before. I always had little crushes on a few different girls but nothing serious by any means. I never had a girlfriend and never truly liked anybody in a deep way.

That would most certainly change on my exchange trip.

The year before my exchange I had a good friend in the same district I was in who went abroad on his exchange in one of the European countries. Let's call this friend Alan. He was a good friend of mine so he told me a lot about what he experienced over there. Alan had also never had a girlfriend before his exchange but that would change for him as well. He ended up getting really close with this girl and ended up dating her toward the last few months of his exchange. They ended up dating and she decided to come back home with him and spend the summer with him in America. Alan really liked this girl, so he was super excited to have her come back with him because he was not ready to say goodbye. This girl came back and his family kindly opened their home to her for the whole summer. Long story short this girl was completely and utterly rude to his family and did not appreciate anything they did for her. She was unappreciative and didn't want to do anything else but stay home and watch Netflix. They offered to take her out and the one time she agreed to go out and have a family dinner, she threw a fit and cursed out the waiter. His parents were completely heartbroken and disappointed that they couldn't get her to simply enjoy herself without locking herself in her room. Rotary knew about the situation as well. The girl finally left back home at the end of the summer when I was about to begin my exchange and so every time I spoke with Rotary or Alan's parents, they all told me the same thing. "Do not fall in love". They repeated it over and over again until I assured them I had never even liked anyone before and was not ready to settle especially in my year abroad. I was completely convinced I would not fall in love or find love in my life for a while.

I was wrong.

Nine days into my exchange everyone from my district met up in a nearby city so we could all meet each other for the first time and have our first official rotary meeting together to go over the rules and expectations of the year. Everyone had just gotten out of their cars and was introducing themselves to each other in the parking lot. I was being as charismatic as I could and went out of my way to get to know every single exchange student there. I was introducing myself to everyone and once I was done talking to someone I was looking around to see who I hadn't met yet. I was looking around for a few seconds, and at about 30 feet away (10 meters) I see the most beautiful girl I had ever seen in my entire life. And I kid you not time froze, and everyone became a blur as I was looking at this girl. For the first time, I was actually nervous to talk to one of the exchange students. After about 30 min I finally mustered up the courage to talk to her and I introduced myself to her. She was from South Africa.

I really liked this girl from the start, and she didn't like me back. I never told her how I felt, but we became friends and stayed in contact for the next couple of weeks. I didn't see her much because she lived in a city about an hour away from mine. Three weeks later in late September, we had our Rotary Inbound Orientation down south in Napoli. This was a 4-day trip down in Napoli and Pompeii where all exchange students in Italy came together in one place to learn the rules and expectations of the year while getting to meet all other exchange students from all over the country. This trip consisted of a 14-hour bus ride to Napoli, one whole day in Napoli, a whole day in Pompeii, and the 14-hour bus ride back home.

Coming into this trip this girl and I were nothing more than friends. I knew she didn't have the same feelings back towards me and I was really sad about it. But on this trip, everything changed. I can't tell you the exact moment everything changed. It was many little things that occurred that made us become real close and allowed us to connect on a much deeper level. The feelings we felt towards each other intensified and as a result, we were just considered best friends after that trip.

After talking a lot after that trip, we stayed up till 4:00 am on a Wednesday night just texting each other back and forth and at the end of the night I somehow had the guts to tell her how I felt about her. I told her how I felt, because I knew my time was limited with her, and I could not sit around wasting time wondering 'what if'. So, I told her how I felt about her and to my surprise, she said she felt the same way. There was no other moment in my life that compared to the feelings I felt when she told me that.

At this point, it was the beginning of October and for the next few months we constantly texted and kept in touch as much as we could since we didn't live in the same city. Unfortunately, as I said in a previous chapter, our district was really strict with traveling alone without permission so I only got to see her about twice a month through events Rotary allowed. She was always on my mind, but I knew how important it was to not let it affect my experience at school and with my friends. I had a couple of exchange student friends who fell in love, got a boyfriend, and never did anything else except hang out with that one person. Looking back on it, it was definitely a good thing that we didn't live in the same city because I was still able to experience everything with everyone else by going out with my friends and meeting new people.

My time with this girl was great. It could not have been any better actually. I liked her so much, and I was living on such a high. But there was one major problem....

This girl was from South Africa. In South Africa school starts in January and ends in January. So this girl had already been on her exchange in Italy for 9 months (Since January). And that meant she was leaving in 3 months back to her hometown. That meant I would never see this girl again. I didn't know what to do. My time with her was absolutely perfect, and to have this relationship be ripped apart by life did not seem fair to me. It was October and we both knew in 3 months we would be separated forever.

My approach to the situation was to forget about the time frame, live in the moment, and take full advantage of every opportunity we had together. Her approach was to make sure I did not get too close because she knew it meant it would be even harder to say goodbye and would have a greater effect on us when the time came. As time went on we tried not to think about it. But the time inevitably came, and trying not to think about the problem was only putting a Band-Aid on it and not completely fixing it. There was no right thing to do at the moment. One of the hardest things in life is finally finding someone you truly care about that feels the same towards you, and the reason you get separated is because of life's situational circumstances, not even because you chose to. I had finally found someone I had feelings for. Feelings

120

that I had never felt in my life, and in a short while, our time together would only become a memory, and I had to somehow learn how to live without her in my life anymore.

We spent the last couple weeks together as much as we could before she left. I tried not to think about her leaving, but every time I did, I felt like a piece of me was getting destroyed. I always had this awful feeling in my stomach that I would get when thinking about it and I could not get it to go away. Those last few weeks I had many sleepless nights, shed many tears, and was very depressed. My host family knew it and my friends did as well. It affected my daily mood, and I couldn't control how I felt.

The day finally came where I would see this girl for the last time in my life and had to say goodbye. I didn't know if I would ever see this girl ever in my life. But the whole time I could not help but think "What are the chances that the only girl I could ever see myself spending the rest of my life with, just so happened to live across the world from me."

We had our final dinner as a district to say farewell to the few girls leaving back home to South Africa and Australia. We ate our dinner and everyone said their goodbyes. All the host families, exchange students, Rotarians, and friends all shared their turn in giving their goodbyes; and the last person she said goodbye to was me. As soon as she looked at me to say goodbye, everyone walked away to give us time alone. All the exchange students and Rotarians knew we had a thing together even though we tried to keep quiet about it since it was against the rules, but they respected our time together and would at least give us some time to talk before we said one last goodbye to each other. So, everyone gave us our space and immediately left the restaurant. I took a deep breath before having to do the hardest thing I would ever have to do in my life. I thanked her for all the great times together, all the unforgettable memories, all the feelings I had never felt before, and all the love she poured into me. We started tearing up, and then I looked her in the eye and for the first time in my life I said to her "I love you."

It was the hardest thing I had to do. Life works in mysterious ways. So, maybe one day our paths will cross again and we can reunite and catch up on all the good times of our lives that happened when we were apart. I had no option but to continue on with my life in Italy, and she went back home and continued her life she left on pause for a year. We stayed in touch, but not as much as you would think. We are both very passionate people about life, and truly live it to the fullest. Dwelling on things we could not change was not something we wanted to affect us. So we carried on with our lives, but it was by far harder for me to do than her. I'm not too sure, but she was probably my first true love, and I did not know how to recover from that.

To this day, I still have not felt the same about someone the way I did about this girl during my exchange. I still have not had a girlfriend, or have even come close to getting into a relationship. But she is happy with her life and I am happy with mine right now. We are still friends and catch up every once in a while. It's crazy how life works sometimes. Never doubt, what life can offer you. The last thing I expected to happen on my exchange, was this. Nevertheless, I learned from it, and am blessed to have had the opportunity to feel the same way millions of people feel toward another individual every day. The whole process from beginning to end was definitely the most difficult, yet the most rewarding circumstance that I have single-handedly ever experienced. And for that, I am eternally grateful.

Chapter 10: The 4 D's

Ok. Here it is. The topic everyone loves to talk about. We love it because breaking these rules makes us feel alive. Like we're actually experiencing something worthwhile. Like that instant adrenaline rush of dopamine in your brain by doing something rebellious makes you feel unstoppable and invincible. It is perfectly normal through the eyes of an exchange student, to break these rules, but before I begin to give my take on them I would like to say first.

I DO NOT, IN NO WAY, ENCOURAGE OR CONDONE ANYONE TO GO AND BREAK THESE RULES FOR THE CONSEQUENCES ARE REAL AND COULD, IN FACT, SEND YOU HOME AND RUIN YOUR EXCHANGE YEAR FOREVER.

That being said, breaking these rules are inevitable for most and therefore I must go over them to make sure, if you do in fact break them, you do them safely and in a controlled and moderate manner. I am talking about this because I am here to help you from the perspective from someone who was in your shoes not to long ago, and in order to help you I must be realistic in knowing all these rules might be broken by you even if you are not one to do them in your native country. So let's begin.

First of all, I know every country has different D's, but the ones I was told to follow were these:

No drinking

No drugs

No dating (or sexual activity)

No driving

Other countries might have other ones like no defacing (which is piercing your body or getting tattoos) but that's beyond the point as it all ties in together.

These rules and consequences are very real, and if you believe that the idea of you getting sent home is farfetched and will never happen to you, then let me be the first to tell you: you are wrong. I personally know many people who have been sent home during their exchange and have even heard many stories about it as well. Some districts are more lenient than others when it comes to the rules, and some are extremely strict about them. I would not take my chances if I were you. Your exchange is too valuable to risk through poor behavior and decisions.

The first rule I want to go over is the most common one:

1. No drinking.

This rule is very controversial because it has a lot to do with where you do your exchange. For example, I believe districts in the U.S are more strict with this rule being that the drinking age is 21 as opposed to European countries where people grow up with wine and beer as part of their culture, and people start drinking from a younger age. So exchange students that go to countries that are more lenient on their drinking policy might experience more drinking. But that's not where the problem lies. The problem lies when the exchange student overdoes the drinking. For example, going out and getting too drunk and coming home to their family absolutely wasted in the middle of the night. It's the behavior and decisions you make when you are very intoxicated that has led to the majority of students I've witnessed get sent home.

If you are smart with your alcohol and don't overdo it, you'll most likely be fine if you can control yourself up until the point you fall asleep, or are in a safe environment. The pattern I found to be the problem for many of the exchange students, was that many of them did not know how to behave themselves when they did start drinking. They started doing very stupid things. Things I would never imagine myself doing, even if I was as drunk as they were. This is because I realized many of the exchange students that would act very different when they had even only had the slightest to drink were acting like this because they were the ones that weren't used to drinking before in their native country back home. And rightfully so, because most exchange students are in fact around sixteen or seventeen years old, which is about the time an average teenager from my experience (in America) starts heavily drinking. It's like what I experienced in college as well. All my friends in college that ended up being the wildest and hardest to control on a night out were the ones that never drank in high school. They become exposed to all the drinking opportunities around them and go way too far then what they are capable of, and end up making stupid mistakes because they are too drunk to control themselves.

Therefore, in order to fix this you must keep this in mind - You must know yourself and have great self-awareness. Know what you are capable of. If you know you can't control yourself very well, or don't even know how you would act if you drank more than what you're used to, then it's simple. Don't do it. By taking a step back and simply asking yourself if you are comfortable enough to have a drink or keep drinking you might very well save yourself from doing something you can deeply regret, that could send you home.

All that being said, it would be hypocritical of me however to tell you to keep a tight leash on yourself when it comes to going out and drinking with your friends, because I too got drunk many times during my exchange. I let myself loose and went out with my friends almost every weekend. However, I'll tell you this: I was always very cautious of when I drank because I knew my first host family didn't allow it, and my Rotary district was very strict on it as well. I learned very quickly early on, that they do not mess around when it came to drinking on exchange. (I talk more about this in the "My Experience" section). I don't want you not to drink I just want you to be very cautious and be aware of the consequences if you were to get caught. Some of my best memories on my exchange were when I had been drinking with friends in the city center or at clubs/bars. I would only do this however, when I was almost sure I wasn't going to get caught.

Drinking could make your exchange more fun, for sure. Everyone knows that. Especially when you're with your friends that you're really close with. Just be very careful where you do it, when you do it, and how much you're doing it. I found some of the times during my exchange that the burden of worrying of getting caught drinking was far greater than my desire to drink that night that I just decided not to drink instead. That's how cautious I was. But I was smart with it. Like if I was in another city with exchange students and I knew we weren't going to get caught then I would let myself go and have a great time. It's all about having a balance and being

126

aware of your surroundings. If you can understand the policy of your host family, your exchange program, and understand the situation of the area you are drinking in then you can make your decision on whether you should drink or how much to drink based off that. Be smart, don't let the reason you get sent home be because you drank more than you should have one night out with friends that wasn't even that special anyways.

2. No drugs

No drugs is basically the same thing as I suggested with no drinking. Don't do it if you're not sure how you're going to act, and definitely don't do it if there's a chance you can get caught. Getting caught with drugs in almost any circumstance is worse than getting caught with alcohol. Therefore, the consequences are worse and your exchange program will have little sympathy for you if you get caught doing drugs.

The drug most people get caught doing is smoking weed. With weed, it can be very easy to tell if you have been smoking due to the physical signs that show you have been smoking weed. Even though you may think you're acting perfectly normal people can still smell it on you, and your eyes can even turn bloodshot red. Your behavior changes as well, and your perception of reality changes. So when you think you might be ok, people will know something is off with you. Don't take any chances, especially if you know you're going back home to your host family that night. I might have only smoked a couple of times during my year abroad, even though it was presented to me many times, because I was too paranoid of getting caught and I did not trust myself to be completely careful. Be smart, and if you're second guessing on whether you should do it, save yourself the anxiety and paranoia and don't do it.

3. No dating

I basically covered this in the previous chapter, but the reason this is a rule is because many times before, exchange students started dating abroad and it ruined relationships with their family, the exchange officers, and their friends. Love is a drug, if you have experienced it, you know. It will make you behave in a way that you normally wouldn't. It can be the best thing you have ever experienced BUT it can also ruin your experience as whole abroad when you look back on it. Especially the experience of your host family if you are never spending time with them because of this other person. If you do decide to date, do it in moderation and don't let it affect the relationships you have with your family and friends.

This rule also covers sexual activity. There have been cases before as well where exchange students have gotten pregnant or got other people pregnant. You can imagine how awful this is. Please watch out for this, because this will not only ruin your exchange, but can greatly alter your life back home as well. If you do decide to do this, be smart and be safe with it! Always be safe, that is the number one priority.

4. No driving

This isn't as big of an issue as the others rules, but it needs to be mentioned as well. Driving in a foreign country where you are unfamiliar with the car you're driving, the roads, and the street signs is never a good idea. You not only put yourself at risk of harm, but risk of other people in the car with you or on the road. Even if you are confident in your driving skills this is still a bad idea because if you get in a wreck, even if it's completely the other person's fault, you will still get in a lot of trouble because you weren't supposed to be behind the wheel in the first place. Then, your exchange program will learn about this because of the legal issues and liabilities and you will be sent home, even if you did nothing wrong. You can't predict what will happen in the car so just don't get behind the wheel.

All these precautions aside. These experiences are very much a part of the exchange as a whole, and I'm sure your exchange program would love to see you have no part in them whatsoever. You are however, in the experimental stage of your life where all you are going to what to do is try new things. You might be persuaded to do some things you wouldn't normally do back home, and that's perfectly fine. Try new things and let yourself go a little bit. As long as you don't ruin the peace of mind of someone else or put someone else in danger, and are ready to face any consequence that may come your way, then do whatever you like. Just be sure to not do anything stupid, and always think out the situation before you commit to something.

Summary:

- If you do in fact break the rules, do them in a safe and controlled manner.

- The consequences to these rules are very real. If you believe getting sent home is something that can't happen to you, you're wrong.

- If you know you won't get caught and are aware of the consequences if you do, then let yourself go a little bit. Try new things and have fun, just don't ruin the peace of mind of other people or do anything stupid.

My experience:

I'd first like to start off by saying I broke all the rules the first month of being on my exchange. Some might think it's cool to go out and drink and do all the things you are told not to do, but it very well could cost you your exchange year.

It almost did for me.

As I mentioned in the previous chapter, all exchange students in Italy met for our Rotary Inbound Orientation meeting in late September, three weeks after I arrived in Italy. These four days and three nights in this Orientation were arguably the best few days on my exchange. Never had I experienced so much fun and excitement being around people I loved so much, in such a beautiful place. We were all staying at a nice hotel in Napoli together and always hung out as much as we could. The first full day consisted of touring the city and having a few short meetings covering the guidelines and expectations they had for us throughout the year. We took chartered buses around famous historical monuments and cathedrals. We ate good traditional Neapolitan food like Cannoli and Granitas (an icy Italian slush-like drink). A few times throughout the day, the Rotarians let us roam around the markets on our free time and get food and buy souvenirs. During this time, we all thought it was a good idea to buy a few bottles of alcohol to take back home to the hotels so we could finally all drink together and have even more fun. We knew we had a little music concert the Rotarians had planned for us outside of our hotel the following night and tried to stock up enough for both nights. So we bought a few bottles, hid them in our backpacks, and took them home so we could end the day getting drunk and having even more fun together. Luckily, they didn't check our backpacks so we got the bottles to the hotel safe and sound.

Everything seemed to be running smoothly, and it seemed like this was going to be the perfect night. When we got back to the hotel, a few of the girls texted me and some other exchange students to go to their room so we could open the wine bottles and the other drinks to start the drinking festivities. We played a few games and chugged a lot of wine. I'm not going to lie I was having the time of my life. I was with my favorite people in the world, in my favorite place in the world, and all we are doing is living in the moment and laughing all together. After a while of drinking there, a Brazilian girl in my district texted me to come to her room and drink with them and all the other Brazilians and Latin American girls. I went, and there were a bunch of exchange students there, all drinking as well. We decided to play a card game which required us to sit in a circle.

Right before the game started, we were all just sitting in the circle laughing and talking loud. Suddenly, I see everyone's head turn to the door and the next thing I noticed was the Brazilian girl to my left putting her vodka bottle on my lap very quickly for no reason. I looked down at the bottle in between my legs then looked up at her very confused. She was looking at the door, so I turn to the door and in complete shock see a Rotarian officer staring directly at me with the bottle in my lap.

At this moment, I had no words. I was a little drunk and confused. The exchange students around me either hid the bottles somewhere near them or ran into the restroom or behind the beds. I was probably the first person he saw with a bottle so he singled me out quick which gave everyone enough time to hide the other bottles.

My first thought was there was no way this is happening. Right? Like there is no way I am going to get in trouble for this. I just had one of the best days of my life touring the city with the best people I know, and I have had the most perfect three weeks of my life since arriving to Italy. I thought everything was going to be ok and that I could talk myself out of it. But I quickly realized that wasn't the case.

This guy looks at me, points directly at me and screams with the most intimidating voice I had ever heard, "YOU!" My first thought is, "Oh sh*t". I get up really scared and try to get myself out of the situation by explaining how I was just there hanging out with everyone else, and the drink he saw wasn't mine. But this guy was not having it. He kept shouting at me and cutting me off from speaking. Not only did he not want to hear what I had to say, but I'm pretty sure he couldn't understand anyways. He didn't speak English, and probably only understood a little, but he didn't care what I had to say. He just kept asking me for my name over and over, but before I gave it to him I was trying to explain the situation. But he persisted, "NO. NO. YOUR NAME. WHAT IS YOUR NAME?" I eventually gave it to him, because there was no running away from the situation. We still had 2 days together and we're all staying in the same hotel anyways so I couldn't avoid him. After I gave him my name, he tried to take a picture of me to show all the Rotarians when he reported back to them. I kept covering my face because I didn't want him to take the pictures, I was too scared and didn't want to get sent home.

So there we are exchanging words right outside the room and all the other exchange students are scared out of their minds too, because they think they are going to get in trouble as well. Some rush back to their rooms as quickly as possible, and the others stayed in the restroom or anywhere else they could where they couldn't be seen. I am scared out of my mind right now, and this guy starts telling me, "I'm sorry pack your bags. You are going home tomorrow. You are leaving back home to America tomorrow, pack your bags now." I was like there is no way this is happening. I was speechless. I didn't know what to say. All I wanted to do was cry in a hole. I had never felt this way before. I felt like my life was over. How am I going to explain to my parents and all my other friends who expected me to be gone for a year that only after three weeks of my exchange I was going to be sent back home? I wasn't even enrolled in school or anything that I could go back to. I literally felt like my life was going to be over. I do not wish those emotions I felt on anybody, ever.

The Rotarian left back to bed and was going to immediately report me first thing the next morning because it was too late at night and everybody else was already asleep. I had no idea what to do or where to go. I wanted to try and fix the problem, but I couldn't. I immediately called my South African and Australian friends asking for help. I tried telling them everything that happened. I told them the whole thing as quickly as I could. They could sense the fear and frustration in my voice so they called me over to their room to explain everything that happened in detail. I rushed to their room freaking out and they did a very good job of comforting me and giving me all the possible scenarios of what could happen. The Australians and South Africans had already been there since January (9 months), so they already had established relationships with the Rotarians in our district, and laid out a list of things that could happen to me going forward. After about an hour of freaking out, I started calming down thanks to them and we all decided it would be best for me to wake up really early and try to find our personal district Youth Exchange Officer (the head guy in charge of our own district) before the other Rotarian talked to him first. I wanted him to hear everything from me, so I could apologize and tell him personally I screwed up and that it would never happen again.

I went back to my room that night and just laid down on my bed staring at the ceiling with a billion thoughts running through my mind. That was probably the longest night I have ever had in my life. I laid in bed there with no one else but my thoughts and the idea that I could be getting sent home back to the United States the very next day.

I woke up the next morning and hoped that everything that happened was a dream, but it wasn't. I got dressed quickly and was the first one to arrive at the cafeteria where everyone was going to have breakfast. I waited for him there for about half an hour and finally saw him walk down the stairs. I explained everything to him and deeply apologized for my actions. He was very disappointed, and I begged him not to send me home. I told him nothing like this would ever happen again and kept apologizing. He told me he would talk it over with the rest of the district later and even with my district back home, and would let me know what they decided after the trip.

At the end of the trip, right before we left back home on our chartered bus he pulled me aside and told me they would not send me home this time. THANK GOD. I was incredibly lucky. But he said, if anything else were to happen like this for the rest of the year, even the smallest slip-up, I would be sent home no questions asked.

I had never felt more relieved in my entire life immediately after hearing that news. I vowed to be the best exchange student I possibly could and try to make up for that terrible mistake. I ended up getting on his good side, and was able to make a good name for myself throughout the Rotary community. I got interviewed for the city news a couple of times, came out in the city newspaper for my accomplishments as an exchange student, and created many travel videos of my exchange on YouTube that spread throughout social media and put my Rotary district on the map. This helped the reputation of the district, and persuaded many other Italian students to apply to become an exchange student. I made up for it as best I could in the long run, but it still didn't fix the mistake I made.

This was one of the worst feelings I had ever experienced in my entire life. I was that close to getting sent home because I wanted to have fun one night. If I could go back and do it all over, I would have never put myself in that situation from the start. So next time you decide to drink on your exchange, ask yourself first: "Is it worth it?"

Chapter 11: Saying Goodbye

This is it. This is where the chapter ends. The day you thought and wished would never come. The end to an amazing story full of unforgettable memories, genuine friendships, and lifestyle you wish you were born into. This is the weirdest feeling you will ever have. Your stomach aches and you wish upon anything you could go back to the beginning and start over again. But a year has passed and there you are, waiting to return to a whole other world than the one you've lived in for the last few months. You will soon fight the tears and give hugs and goodbyes to the people who have meant the most to you lately. The people who at one point didn't know anything about you, and yet agreed to open their homes and hearts to you. The people you were randomly put in classes with and who later became your new best friends. The people who have shown you cultures and religions and parts of the world you'd never seen before. The people who helped you find yourself.

You are about to leave this life you built up over the last year, and it is time to let go now. In a few days you will come into town and see the familiar roads and buildings and it will seem like last time you were here was in a dream. You will see the people you had to let go of a year ago, and you will slowly get back to the normal life you used to live. You will soon start to realize how much things have changed - how much you have changed. You will desperately try to hold on to every person and every memory from your host country, but sooner or later you will have to realize that you have a lot to leave behind.

You will take down your pictures and pack up your clothes. You will see your town one last time before you get on the flight back home to your home country. No more spontaneous trips. No more coffee in the city center. No more sleepovers with your best friends. No more speaking your second language every day, and no more people making fun of your accent. You will put your memories aside for right now. It's time to leave this fantasy of a dream and get back to the real world. The world where you grew up and became who you are today. This year has changed you a lot, and you will have to dig deep inside to find the strength to adjust to the big changes in your life - again. Pretty soon you will walk into your old house and your old bedroom. Every emotion will pass through you as you reflect on your life and how much it has changed in the last few months. You will unpack your things and you will have dinner with your family, and you will go back to reality.

So how do you deal with this heartbreaking goodbye? There are a few things you can do to help ease the pain and distract your mind.

1. Stop and smell the roses

You cherish it while you're still living it, so when you do go home you can go home with full closure. I want you to become deeply aware of the fact that this day will come a lot sooner than you think. Have that in the back of your mind, so you can cherish every single little mundane thing you do on your exchange. That coffee date with the other exchange students, the walk to school with your classmates, and that hour long talk after dinner with your host family. These are the little things that bring your whole exchange back together to make it so special to you. Don't forget to stop and smell the roses. Time will pass you by, and if you're not careful you are going to regret not cherishing every second of it.

Put earphones in, and listen to music on your walk to school. Look at the people passing by, each one living a life as vivid and complex as your own. Each one populated with their own ambitions, friends, routines, and craziness. Look at the buildings surrounding you. You might never see these kinds of buildings again. The architecture, faded paint, and artistic graffiti. Cherish those feelings and realize how lucky you are to be able to live the life you are currently living. Repeat to yourself while jamming to the awesome music you're listening to, "I am in freaking [Italy]! I am in freaking [Italy] and I love my life so much. How did I get so lucky!?" Remind yourself how lucky you are, and that you are in a beautiful country with people you might never see again. This will bring you back to the present moment, and will keep you from getting to ahead of yourself and taking each day for granted.

2. Be prepared for the mind shift.

Realize when you get home you will not be the same person you were when you left a year ago. You might not feel you have changed, but you did. You might think everyone around you back home has changed and they just don't understand you anymore. This is not the case. The one who has changed is you - and for the better. Don't expect them to understand you. You just lived and experienced a whole new life in a year. No normal human being can understand what you went through without actually experiencing it themselves. You have to be prepared to have matured everyone out. This will be frustrating, because your friends will still be as close-minded as before. You can't expect them to change and adapt to your new way of thinking, and you can't blame anyone for not understanding you. All you can do is continue to grow yourself and maybe even find a new group of friends with the same mindset as you. There will always be people that understand the new you. Whether it was your friends you left behind, or new people you will have to meet.

The common mistake here is that people and things seem to change when you get back, but no one realizes it was them that changed. If you understand this, you won't feel so trapped in your new life, and you can continue to grow into the person you wanted to be your whole life, personally and professionally.

3. Stay involved

Many of us try to find a way to cope with this new way of living in different ways. We want to share our stories and experiences and let everyone know how crazy this last year of our life has been. One huge way we cope with this is by continuously going to our friends and talking to them about our experiences abroad. And rightfully so, correct? I mean every time we do something or hear something that reminds us of a crazy experience we had abroad we are going to want to bring it up because it makes us happy to reminisce on these moments. But what you will realize is that your "friends" will begin to get annoyed of you always bringing up your exchange. They will get frustrated with you and tell you to stop always talking about it. And then you might feel like garbage because you can't even talk to your own friends about the best experience of your life.

Instead, one way I suggest you should cope with this new life is by staying involved in the Youth Exchange community. You are going to want people around you that you can talk to about your experiences. And there is no one else in the world that wants to hear your stories more than people that will soon experience it, or people that have already experienced it and want to re-live those glory days with similar experiences. Stay involved in that community, either through the exchange students you met abroad, or through Facebook and social media group messages. You can talk about your experiences and simultaneously help someone else out with a problem they may be having on their exchange. Help anybody else you can. Get on those groups and tell them what they should and shouldn't do with a particular problem they're having. You can share your past experience through that, and in return, they will learn from you as well.

You can also get involved with the current exchange students in your area or school, and they can become one of your friend groups. If you are back home and your district has new inbound students. Live vicariously through them and have fun with them. You guys can share stories, and while you are re-living your past, you are helping them have a great time on their exchange as well. It's a win-win situation. I made many great friends by doing this. I was always trying to help people that would reach out to me on Instagram or Facebook, and I would also hang out with the exchange students in my school and helped them have a great time on their exchange in my city. In fact, I joined an organization where I became a mentor to the students studying abroad in my University from different countries all around the world. They became my friend group freshman year of College, and I enjoyed every second of it. I lived vicariously through them, and felt the duty to help them have as much fun as possible during their time here in my city.

Staying involved in the exchange community is a good way to help you cope with the fact that you may be depressed coming back home. In a way, it keeps your exchange alive and never-ending. It is just the next chapter to your *Exchange Life*. Giving back the way people gave back to you on your exchange.

These are a few different things to help you deal with the fact that your exchange may be over. If you have never been depressed before, you might experience it now.

Even though it's going to be hard, how lucky are you to have something that makes saying goodbye so hard? This is not a goodbye. This is an "I'll see you later." Because distance means nothing. Not when the person or thing means so much to you. Somehow you will find a way to adjust between the two different worlds you now live in. Your life will carry on, and you will always have that baggage you carry around with you wherever you go for the rest of your life. And that's when you start to realize:

"You build a life for 16 years
And leave it for 10 months
You build a life for 10 months
And leave it forever.
    Which one is harder?"

Summary:

- Become deeply aware with the fact that all this is temporary. You need to stop and cherish every second of it.

- When we get home, home is still the same, but something in our minds has changed, and that changes everything.

- Don't be sad because it's over; be happy because it happened.

My experience:

One of the most important realizations I learned in my life was during my exchange. I was constantly in situations where I felt this weird sensation in my stomach when good things were coming to an end, and I didn't know how to explain it. But I came out with this lesson.

"One of the most bittersweet feelings has to be when you realize how much you're going to miss a moment, while you're still living it."

I always stopped to realize what I was doing at that moment and where I was at in the world, was not normal for my life, or anybody else's life for that matter. I was truly living a fantasy. And when I did realize this I was conscious enough to know it would come to an end pretty soon. Not my exchange but that particular moment. It could have been something as mundane as having an espresso with my best friends right next to the city cathedral or enjoying a train ride with exchange students to a new city. I realized these small little moments meant so much to me. I wanted to grab the moment and never let it go. I obviously knew that was not physically possible, so I began to get this weird feeling in my stomach of bitter sweetness. I was enjoying the moment so much, that I was going to be sad when it came to an end. I'm sure many of you can relate.

One of my best experiences with this was in Venice, Italy. I was with best exchange student friend, Leo, from Mexico (who I have mentioned before in previous chapters). The reason why I loved Leo so much was that this guy was just as aware as me in the fact that we knew this was an absolute once in a lifetime opportunity and we could not have been more grateful for being in Italy in this time of our lives.

Leo and I wanted to do a trip together. We had only been on our exchange for a few months, but we wanted to go explore a little. My host sister was studying at a University in Venice, and we decided to try and somehow manage a trip together to go stay with her and explore the city. We really wanted to go to Venice, because we hadn't been yet. After talking to our host parents and Rotary, everyone was ok with us going to stay with my sister for a couple of nights because she was part of my host family.

We're finally ready to embark on our trip a couple of weeks later. Leo and I ride the train to Venice together telling stories and catching up with how our exchange was going. We arrive in Venice and my sister meets us at the train station. We are all so happy to be together and especially for me and Leo to see The City on Water with our very own eyes for the first time. We drop off our bags at my sister's place and we all go explore the gorgeous city together. Leo and I were in awe. We were in complete shock that it was just us three together, with no worries, walking through the narrow sidewalks of one of the most beautiful and unique cities on the planet. We were on such a high that nothing could bring us down. We had an absolute blast exploring the city together all day.

After one of the most fun days of our lives exploring the city, we get home, eat dinner and relax. Leo and I had so much fun together we decided to go out again at night and explore this city in the dark because we didn't have enough of it. My sister was ok with it and stayed home to sleep to get ready for school the next day. Leo and

I went out with nothing but our phones and began walking through this maze-like city. This city is basically a maze, all streets look the same and they all lead you back to somewhere you think you've been before, but have actually never seen. We didn't care, we had google map on our phones and knew wherever we went we could always get back home no problem. So we left late at night and walked and talked and explored the streets of Venice.

I want you to imagine walking down these streets with nothing but the sounds of the water hitting the sidewalk and the gondolas rocking in the canals every corner you turned to, feeling nothing but complete bliss. All this combined with your best friend in the world experiencing this with you at the moment. There are not many greater feelings in the world than that right there.

Our only job that night was to get lost. We kept exploring around the city and found many cool things along the way. We found this nice spot of water in between two buildings that had a great view of the city and other boats on the canal. There was a gondola in this little spot and we just hopped in, looked at each other, smiled, and took it all in. We knew what the other one was thinking and we just didn't speak. Our facial expression communicated it all. It was complete bliss.

After a while of hanging inside the gondola, soaking it all in, we decided it might be time to go back home because it was now 1:00 a.m. and we didn't want my sister worrying about us. So we pulled out our phones and mapped our way back to my sister's place. Connection was rough since we were basically in the middle of nowhere with no great service, and we didn't have the best service provider considering we were poor exchange students. I mapped us back home, and my crappy phone went into overdrive trying to find us the directions through google maps. It ended up working so hard, it killed my battery within minutes. My phone died and I was like just like dammit that sucks. No big deal though, I just asked Leo to map us back home. So he took out his phone to map us back home, and his phone did the same thing. It worked really hard to find the connection and killed his battery too. Now both our phones were dead...

I looked up at him, we stared at each other right in the eyes for a couple of seconds second and busted out laughing! There we were, in the middle of this gigantic maze of a city, COMPLETELY lost and no way of getting home. We tried re-tracing our steps back home, but like I said it was dark and every street looked the same. We walked around trying to find home for an hour, but could not find it.

We got exactly what we asked for. To get completely lost with no way of getting home. It was now 3:00 a.m. and after walking around for two hours, we just said screw it and sat down by one of the canals in defeat. We sat there with our legs hanging over the edge, and we just talked. Leo and I were best friends, but it was after this talk that I realized I would NEVER find someone like Leo in my life. We opened up and shared our dreams and aspirations. We talked about where we wanted to live in the future, what business we wanted to start, how we wanted to raise our kids, and what kind of girl we wanted to marry. We found out we would listen to the same YouTube motivational videos back home and we began reciting some motivational quotes that we knew by heart. He would say one and I would jump in and finish his sentence because I had listened to that certain quote hundreds of times before. We instantly clicked and created a new form of friendship I had never experienced before.

There we were with our legs hanging over the water, looking up at the stars and the Milky Way galaxy, just contemplating life. We were sitting there in silence, and I was enjoying every second of it. Then it started to hit me. We were completely stranded and might not make it home tonight, and I started to get a little worried. What if we never made it home, and my sister woke up to see no one there. There was no way she could call us on our phones to communicate with us. She would probably get worried and call my host parents, and then everyone would be freaking out. It was already hard enough to convince them to let me and Leo go on this trip together alone.

All these thoughts started to hit me, and I began to panic a little. But then, Leo said something that spoke volumes to me. It was something I would never forget... He was looking up at the stars and he said in a calm voice, "Bro... We are in freaking Italy...." And I stopped. And I looked at him, and I immediately knew what he was talking about. Why the heck should I be worried? Everything is going to be alright. We were lost, but we were lost in freaking Venice, Italy. I had no reason to be worried. I have my best friend with me in one of the most beautiful cities in the world. I was living the life, and no matter what happened, I knew everything was going to be alright.

So, I looked at him and said it back. "Bro, we are in freaking Italy." And we both smiled the biggest smiles we had ever done in our lives, and we shouted at the top of our lungs in the streets of Venice, Italy.

"WE ARE IN FREAKING ITALY!!!"

We completely forgot about the fact that we might not make it home that night, but we knew everything was going to be ok. That was a feeling of bitter sweetness. We stopped and smelled the roses and continued talking about how freaking lucky we were to be in Venice, Italy. A place where so many people dream of being, and never make it to in their lives. There we were, 18-year-olds, lost in the streets of Venice with nothing but each other. Best friends, living the best life we could possibly imagine for ourselves.

I remembered that quote by Leo since then. It taught me to appreciate the smallest things in my life. Even though it seemed like all was lost we didn't need to worry, because we were in Italy and at the end of the day everything was going to be fine. I can't express the kind of emotion I felt that night with Leo. All I knew was that I didn't want that moment to end. It was complete bliss and that was a moment I will never forget for the rest of my life. Those moments were the moments we all live for. No one can take away those memories from us. All we can do is look back on them and appreciate them for shaping us to who we are today. I will forever be grateful it was Leo by my side that night. I felt a rush of love for him, for the city, for the country, and for the Universe for helping us get lost together and experiencing one of my most fondest memories I have to look back on for the rest of my life.

It was now about 4:30 a.m. and after a while of sitting there and enjoying our company and our life at the moment, we decided to get back up and find our way back home once more. To our complete and utter surprise, we walked down a series of streets and found our way back home in a matter of 10 minutes... It was as if fate had set us up to experience that together, and it decided it was now time to come back home. We learned our lesson, gained our appreciation for our lives together, and were now even more fulfilled than before. And without a problem, found our way back home, to end the night in a perfect way.

We got completely lost, and looking back on it, I am so glad our phones died, or I would have never had that memory and learned that lesson. Nothing else mattered at that moment. It was just Leo, me, the water beneath us, and the stars above us, and we didn't care about anything else. Sometimes it's best to get lost. It might be scary in the moment, but you might definitely learn something from it. I know I did.

I learned the valuable lesson of living in the moment and truly appreciating every day and every moment to the best of my ability. From that point on, I found myself in situations where I would remind myself how grateful I was to be there. This helped me absorb as much of my exchange as I could, and I left with that ultimate bittersweet feeling, knowing there was nothing more I could have done, to live the best year I have ever lived in my life.

Can you do me a favor

Thank you for buying and reading my book. I really hope you enjoyed it! I'm confident that following what I've laid out will help you not only survive in your host country, but thrive. By applying what's in these chapters you can transform your life abroad and live the best life you could have possibly imagined for yourself in your host country.

Before you go I have a small favor to ask. Would you take a minute to write a brief review about this book on Amazon? Reviews are the best way to help this book get noticed, and help many other exchange students that stumble across the book to help them live their dream life abroad as well. I also read every review and will use that feedback to write future revisions too, and future books even that are most suitable for your needs.

Thank you!

And if you ever want to get in contact or stay updated with all my travels here are my social media accounts for you to follow.

Instagram: andyserna
YouTube: Andy Serna
Facebook: Andy Serna
Email: andrew_serna@icloud.com